The
LEGEND
and the
APOSTLE

D0802348

The
LEGEND
and the
APOSTLE

The Battle for Paul
in Story and Canon

by

Dennis Ronald MacDonald

The Westminster Press
Philadelphia

BOOK DESIGN BY ALICE DERR

First edition

Published by The Westminster Press®
Philadelphia, Pennsylvania

PRINTED IN THE UNITED STATES OF AMERICA
9 8 7 6 5 4 3 2 1

Library of Congress Cataloging in Publication Data

MacDonald, Dennis Ronald, 1946–
  The legend and the Apostle.

  Bibliography: p.
  Includes index.
  1. Acts of Paul—Criticism, interpretation, etc.
  2. Bible. N.T. Pastoral Epistles—Criticism, interpretation, etc. 3. Paul, the Apostle, Saint. 4. Bible.
  N.T.—Canon. 5. Women in Christianity—History—Early
  church, ca. 30-600. I. Title.
  BS2880.P4M33 1983   227'.012   82-21953
  ISBN 0-664-24464-5 (pbk.)

To my Mother
Mildred Friend MacDonald

Sicut beatissimam Thecla . . .
de tribus atrocissimis tormentis liberasti,
sic liberare digneris animam hujus servi tui.

Just as you have freed the most blessed Thecla . . .
from three cruel torments,
so also may you deign to free the soul of your servant.

From a prayer said
on St. Thecla's feast day

CONTENTS

ABBREVIATIONS

ACW	Ancient Christian Writers
ANF	Ante-Nicene Fathers
AP	*Acts of Paul*
AT	Aarne-Thompson. Antti Amatus Aarne. *The Types of the Folktale: A Classification and Bibliography.* Second revision tr. and enl. by Stith Thompson. Helsinki: Finnish Academy of Sciences & Letters 1961.
B.C.E	before the common era (= B.C.)
BEvT	Beiträge zur evangelischen Theologie
BG	Berlin Gnostic Codex
BHT	Beiträge zur historischen Theologie
BJRL	*Bulletin of the John Rylands Library,* Manchester
BZ	*Biblische Zeitschrift*
BZNW	Beihefte zur Zeitschrift für die neutestamentliche Wissenschaft
CBQ	*Catholic Biblical Quarterly*
ca.	*circa* (around)
C.E.	common era (= A.D.)
CG	Coptic Gnostic Library
col., cols.	column, columns
CSEL	Corpus scriptorum ecclesiasticorum latinorum
DACL	*Dictionnaire d'archéologie chrétienne et de liturgie*
ed.	edition, edited
fig.	figure
FRLANT	Forschungen zur Religion und Literatur des Alten und Neuen Testaments
GCS	Griechische christliche Schriftsteller
HNT	Handbuch zum Neuen Testament
HTR	*Harvard Theological Review*

JAC	Jahrbuch für Antike und Christentum
JBL	*Journal of Biblical Literature*
JR	*Journal of Religion*
JTS	*Journal of Theological Studies*
Loeb	Loeb Classical Library
LXX	Septuagint
mir., mirs.	miracle, miracles
NEB	New English Bible
n.	note
NPNF	Nicene and Post-Nicene Fathers
n.s.	new series
NTS	*New Testament Studies*
p., pp.	page, pages
PG	J. P. Migne, *Patrologia graeca*
PL	J. P. Migne, *Patrologia latina*
rev.	revision, revised
RSV	Revised Standard Version
SBS	Stuttgarter Bibelstudien
SC	Sources chrétiennes
SE	*Studia Evangelica*
s.v.	*sub verbo* (under the word)
trans.	translation, translated
TU	Texte und Untersuchungen
v., vs.	verse, verses
VC	*Vigiliae christianae*
ZNW	*Zeitschrift für die neutestamentliche Wissenschaft*
ZTK	*Zeitschrift für Theologie und Kirche*

ACKNOWLEDGMENTS

This book was inspired by an assignment for a class at Harvard Divinity School in the spring of 1976. We were to read and compare several texts illustrative of ancient religious attitudes toward asceticism and civil morality. While doing so, I became fascinated by a curious relationship between the *Acts of Paul and Thecla* and the Pastoral Epistles, but I also became frustrated by the failure of scholarship to describe that relationship, a tangle as baffling as the fabled Gordian knot. For the next two years I tried in vain to untangle it and was about to give up when a doctoral student in oral literature at Harvard suggested that my approach was too literary. She suggested I do some reading in folkloristics. I did, and there I found the sword to cut the knot. Whatever contributions this book may make, they are due in large measure to my friends and mentors Helmut Koester and Zeph Stewart, whose class it was, and to Margaret Hiebert, who initiated me into the world of folklore.

I also must acknowledge my debts to Joe Springer, Marion Wenger, John Stanley, Susan Hogan Doty, and the library staffs at Goshen College and The Iliff School of Theology for their assistance in my research. To Gene Tucker of The Candler School of Theology, J. Christiaan Beker of Princeton Theological Seminary, Kent Richards and Andrew Scrimgeour my colleagues at Iliff, Diane Prosser MacDonald my wife, and Cynthia Thompson and James Heaney of Westminster Press I owe thanks for the solicitous, painstaking attention they gave to the manuscript.

Above all, I am indebted to my brother, Peter J. MacDonald, for having applied his expertise in discourse analysis to the stories in the *Acts of Paul*. His attention to detail, his patience and methodological sophistication have profoundly enriched this book. It is appropriate, therefore, to dedicate this to our mother, Mildred Friend MacDonald, who nurtured us physically and spiritually, and whose life—like Thecla's—is a story of freedom found in the service of Christ.

INTRODUCTION

In *The Golden Ass,* by Apuleius (ca. 123–180 C.E.), the character Lucius, who had been turned into an ass by misapplying a magical formula he had learned from a witch, travels in search of an antidote to return him to his natural state. While traveling, he falls into the clutches of bandits who hide him in a cave along with two women, one old and one young. The younger had been kidnapped from her wedding, and was terrified by her captivity lest she lose her lover. To console her the older woman says: "Now let me tell you some old women's tales *(anilibus fabulis)* to make you feel a little better."[1] Then she tells the story of the tribulations Psyche had to face before she married Cupid. At the end of it Lucius says: "I stood close by the girl prisoner listening to this beautiful story, and though it was told by a drunken and half-demented old woman, I regretted that I had no means of committing it to writing."[2]

This is but one example from antiquity of the prominence of women in transmitting oral narrative—especially myths. As in this passage, most of these references are pejorative. In Plato's *Republic,* for instance, Socrates tells his friend Adeimantus that in order to create their utopia they must control the content of the stories women tell their children:

> Then we must first of all, it seems, control the story tellers. Whatever noble story they compose we shall select, but a bad one we must reject. Then we shall persuade nurses and mothers to tell their children those we have selected and by those stories to fashion their minds far more than they can shape their bodies by handling them. The majority of the stories they now tell must be thrown out.[3]

Or again:

> Possibly, however, you regard this as an old wives' tale, and despise it. (Plato, *Gorgias* 527A)
>
> Your stories still remain old wives' tales. (Lucian, *The Lover of Lies* 9)
>
> Poetry is a fable-prating old woman, who has been permitted to invent ... whatever she deems suitable for purposes of entertainment. (Eratosthenes, as paraphrased by Strabo, *Geography* 1, 2, 3, C 16)
>
> For in dealing with a crowd of women ... a philosopher cannot influence them by reason or exhort them to reverence, piety and faith; no, there is need of superstitious fear also, and this is not possible without mythic tales and miracles. (Strabo, *Geography* 1, 2, 8, C 19)

The author of the Pastoral Epistles—1 and 2 Timothy and Titus—stands in this tradition of men who despised "old wives' tales": "Avoid the profane tales told by old women" (1 Tim. 4:7).[4] Most interpreters have taken this verse to be nothing more than stock rhetoric used to vilify the theology of the "false teachers." Hence, some modern translations disguise the reference to women: "Have nothing to do with godless and silly myths" (RSV); "Steer clear of all these stupid Godless fictions" (Phillips). Other translations retain the reference to women but preclude the possibility that the author in fact might have been objecting to women telling stories: "Leave foolish nursery tales alone" (Ronald Knox); "Have nothing to do with those godless myths, fit only for old women" (NEB).

In this book I shall argue that the author of the Pastoral Epistles wrote in Paul's name in order to counteract the image of Paul as given in stories told by women. In Chapter I, I shall show that behind the apocryphal *Acts of Paul,* written between 150 and 190 C.E., lie several earlier oral legends about Paul. Chapter II briefly reconstructs the social values of the legends, which include freedom for women to teach in the church, celibacy, and adamant opposition to Rome. Chapter III shows that the author of the Pastoral Epistles probably knew these legends, objected to their use of Paul's memory to sanction social deviance, and fashioned his pseudo-Pauline letters to present Paul as a social conservative and to silence the tale-telling women. Chapter IV describes how the Pastoral Epistles successfully made their way into the New Testament as authentically Pauline, and Chapter V describes how the legend tradition continued to flourish for centuries in spite of the church's canonizing of the Pastorals by including them in the New Testament. The conclusion discusses the significance of the battle for Paul's memory for the modern church.

This study of the Pastoral Epistles and the *Acts of Paul* is devoted to placing them properly within the development and polarization of Pauline tradition in second-century Asia Minor.[5] I am convinced that the Pastoral Epistles have distorted our image of Paul, even for those of us who recognize them as pseudonymous. Scholars still too often assume that the Pastoral Epistles were more or less standard expressions of Paulinism for post-Pauline churches. But this fails to account for the tremendous diversity of ways the early church remembered the apostle, and consequently we have too often seen the apostle of freedom as the priest of social convention. The domestication of Paul in the Pastoral Epistles was not an inevitable, linear development of the Pauline mission, as is usually assumed.

The alternative view of the apostle does not simply eliminate the Pastoral Epistles from our New Testaments and accept the depiction of Paul in the legends as more authoritative. Rather, we must see both within the context of early debates over the Pauline heritage. If we are to be properly engaged and informed by our religious past, the views of Paul himself and the full range of options chosen by subsequent generations within Pauline tradition should be sorted out. Thus we can learn from their combined experience and from the historical process in which they participated. With all due respect to the author of the Pastoral Epistles, when we read the *Acts of Paul* we recognize that not all Christians in the Pauline circle would have silenced women from teaching, trimmed the order of widows, exhorted slaves to continued servitude, and commanded obedience to Roman authority. We can, in short, no longer assume that the Pastoral Epistles were the rightful second-century heirs of the Pauline legacy. Perhaps it is now time for our own images of Paul and the religious movement that he generated to be shaped not only by the Pastoral Epistles but also by the stories of those unknown raconteurs who lost the battle for Paul's memory.

CHAPTER I

The Oral Legends
Behind the *Acts of Paul*

At the close of the second century the African church father Tertullian complained that some Christians were using the example of a woman named Thecla to legitimate women teaching and baptizing. According to them, she had been commissioned to do so by Paul himself.[1] To oppose those who told the Thecla story, Tertullian claimed that it was merely spun from the imagination of an Asian presbyter who "from love of Paul" had written it in a book falsely bearing the apostle's name. When the presbyter confessed he had done so, Tertullian says, he was deposed from his office. Origen knew this book as the *Acts of Paul* and spoke of it with modest approval.[2] Eusebius' attitude was more tentative, and Jerome, who knew it as the *Journeys of Paul and Thecla,* dismissed it as apocryphal.[3] As the piecemeal textual transmission of the *Acts of Paul* illustrates, the church at large shared Tertullian's disdain for it, perhaps because of its later popularity among heretics.[4] Not until our own century have we known the extent of its contents, not until Carl Schmidt and others established a reliable—if fragmentary—reconstruction of the text by piecing together scraps of Greek and Coptic papyri.[5] It now appears that the *Acts of Paul* consisted of a series of stories about Paul's adventures in Syria, Asia Minor, and Greece, and ended with his martyrdom in Rome. From the contents of this reconstruction it is clear that Tertullian was correct in placing its origin in Asia Minor and in attributing it to the hand of a member of the great church. The author clearly was not either Gnostic or Marcionite.[6]

But Tertullian undoubtedly was wrong in claiming that the author concocted these stories from his own fantasies, for several of them clearly are traditional and probably extend back into the first century.[7] The people whom Tertullian opposed did not learn the story of Thecla from reading the *Acts of Paul;* rather, they simply were repeating an ancient Christian legend which the author of the *Acts of Paul* likewise knew and incorporated into his book along with other legends. He paid for his innocence with the loss of his presbyterial office.

In this chapter we shall attempt to determine the extent of oral tradition behind the *Acts of Paul.* Doing so, we sail into waters largely uncharted and full of perils for the unwary and overzealous adventurer.[8] Oral and written narratives are too closely related to be easily divided and so most conclusions about the oral strata behind a text must be tentative.[9] From the start, therefore, we must abandon all hope of rediscovering the "oral text" of any of the stories. Barring further manuscript discoveries, the only text of them we shall ever have is the one written down by the Asian presbyter. On the other hand, we can discover the general oral content of the stories by demonstrating their independence from written sources, their folkloric themes, and their circulation apart from the *Acts of Paul.* And we can discover their oral form or structure by determining the extent to which they adhere to generally recognized conventions of oral narrative.

Our investigation will be restricted to three stories in the *Acts of Paul* which together comprise almost three fourths of the reconstructed book: the Thecla story, the Ephesus story (sometimes known as the story of Paul and the baptized lion), and the martyrdom story. By treating only these stories I am making no tacit judgment concerning the composition histories of the others. I have chosen to concentrate on these three because (1) each of the stories is attested by Tertullian, Origen, or Jerome, and therefore undoubtedly was present in the ancient versions of the *Acts of Paul,* (2) each story follows a narrative pattern not found in any other stories in the *Acts of Paul,* and (3) each story has its own integrity—that is, each has a discrete beginning and ending and has content independent of other parts of the *Acts of Paul.*

No analysis of a story—no matter how comprehensive—can capture its subtlety, color, or intensity. To know a story is to have heard or read it; consequently, the reader is strongly urged to read them in *New Testament Apocrypha,* Vol. 2.[10] Even though reading these stories is not mandatory for understanding the rest of this book, where they will in any event appear in paraphrase, those who do read them no doubt will understand more fully, and, what is more important, will experience three of the most delightful of all early Christian tales.

THE ORAL CONTENT OF THE STORIES

THE THECLA STORY

The longest story in the *Acts of Paul* tells of the fate of Thecla, a young and beautiful woman who, on the eve of her wedding to Thamyris, a wealthy Iconian, hears Paul preach and converts to his message of resurrection and chastity. When Thamyris fails to woo her back from Paul, he and Thecla's mother, Theocleia, take her to the governor, who orders her brought to the theater naked to be burned at the stake. A hailstorm extinguishes the fire, and Thecla is saved. She finds Paul, tells him she will cut her hair short—i.e., like a man's—and follow him if he will baptize her. But Paul is not yet sure of her commitment. Together they go to Antioch of Pisidia, where another frustrated would-be lover condemns Thecla before the governor. In spite of the protests of the women of the city, including a Queen Tryphaena, she is thrown naked to the beasts, baptizes herself in a pool of seals, is saved by a series of miracles, sews her mantle so that she will look like a man, and flees to Paul, who ordains her to teach.

One of the most persuasive reasons for thinking the story came from oral tradition is Tertullian's reference to those who told it to legitimate the ministries of women. Furthermore, the story is laden with folkloric commonplace. Beautiful, nubile women, frustrated lovers, journeys, perils, and miraculous rescues are the storyteller's stock-in-trade.[11]

Ludwig Radermacher has argued that the legend of Thecla is a Christian adaptation of the ancient legend of Hippolytus in which Phaedra tries to seduce Hippolytus to break his vow of chastity.[12] Although it is unlikely that the legends of Hippolytus and Thecla are as closely related as Radermacher thought, or that the legend ultimately derived from the cults of mother earth goddesses, he does show brilliantly that the Thecla story is a variation of a tale type that was popular in Greek antiquity from the fifth century B.C.E. when Euripides wrote his *Hippolytus* until the fifth century C.E. when Christians told the legend of Pelagia of Tarsus, who was killed for not becoming mistress to the emperor.[13] He also shows that some of the Hellenistic novelists employed the tale type.[14]

But there is another legend that is even more similar to the Thecla story than the legend of Hippolytus. A Latin author named Hyginus epitomized and translated a Greek work which was a treasure trove of oral lore. It contained two hundred and seventy-seven *fabulae*. Hyginus' translation was made before 207 C.E. and probably sometime in the second century, which makes it roughly contemporary with the *Acts of Paul*.[15] One of these stories is about a woman named Hagnodice, who allegedly was the first Greek woman to be a physician. Apparently the story was told to legitimate the existence of women in that profession, just as the story of Thecla was used to support a role for women in teaching and baptizing, according to Tertullian. Furthermore, the prominence of women and the antagonism for men in the story may indicate that it was told primarily by women.

> The ancients didn't have obstetricians, and as a result, women because of modesty perished. For the Athenians forbade slaves and women to learn the art of medicine. A certain girl, Hagnodice, a virgin, desired to learn medicine, and since she desired it, she cut her hair, and in male attire came to a certain Herophilus for training. When she had learned the art, and had heard that a woman was in labor, she came to her. And when the woman refused to trust herself to her, thinking that she was a man, she removed her garment to show that she was a woman, and in this way she treated women. When the doctors saw that they were not admitted to women, they began to accuse Hagnodice, saying that "he" was a seducer and corruptor of women, and that the women were pretending to be ill. The Areopagites, in session, started to condemn Hagnodice, but Hagnodice removed her garment for them and showed that she was a woman. Then the doctors began to accuse her more vigorously, and as a result the leading women came to the Court and said: "You are not husbands, but enemies, because you condemn her who discovered safety for us." Then the Athenians amended the law, so that free-born women could learn the art of medicine.[16]

Both Hagnodice and Thecla are virgins who cut their hair, wear male dress, study under a revered male teacher, and ultimately perform male tasks. In both stories the women are accused of destroying households, are forced to expose their bodies to hostile men, and are protected by other women. The similarities between these stories cannot be attributed to a common literary source, nor to the dependence of one book on the other. Both clearly were oral tales about women who broke traditional barriers against their professional pursuits. Perhaps it is worth noting that later traditions about Thecla made her into a divine healer who robbed male physicians of their clients.[17]

Further evidence that the story of Thecla circulated orally comes from a reference in the story to Queen Tryphaena. There was, in fact, a queen of Pontus named Tryphaena, a contemporary of Paul and a distant relative of the reigning Claudians, just as the *Acts of Paul* says. The correspondence does not prove the historical reliability of the *Acts of Paul*, William M. Ramsay has argued,[18] for the *Acts of Paul* says she lived in Antioch of Pisidia and was a convert to Christianity, while other evidence indicates she made her home in Cyzicus and was a priestess of Livia.[19] Nevertheless, it is unlikely that a story about her would have been created late in the second century when the *Acts of Paul* was written. Perhaps the memories of these two respected Anatolian women, Thecla and Tryphaena, were joined together in oral tradition by Christians who identified this queen with the Tryphaena mentioned in Rom 16:12 as one who had worked with Paul. This suggestion is strengthened if, as many scholars think, Romans 16 originally was destined for Ephesus.[20]

Furthermore, there is no necessary connection between denying the historicity of the legend about Thecla—which we must—and denying her existence. On the contrary, her existence would help explain the origin of the legend.[21] But whether Thecla was the name of a historical person or merely the name of a legendary heroine, no author from the first millennium of the church ever doubted Thecla's existence. They consistently numbered her among the early saints, and even occasionally called her a protomartyr and an apostle.[22] Jerome (fourth century) lists Thecla among the saints in one passage, while challenging the credibility of the *Acts of Paul* in another.[23] Surely this rejection of the book and reception of the legend suggests that her memory persisted independently of the *Acts of Paul*. Perhaps oral tradition was also a source for the life of Thecla written by Athanasius (mid-fourth century),[24] and for the variations of the legend in Pseudo-Chrysostom (fifth century)[25] and in the textual transmission of the *Acts of Paul and Thecla*.[26] There can be no doubt, however, that she became a popular subject in oral tradition and in hagiography even beyond the fifth century.[27] She was so popular that by the year 375 a monastery in Seleucia, Isauria, had been dedicated to her. Literary and archaeological evidence attests a widespread Thecla cult which we shall discuss in some detail in Chapter V.[28]

Cumulatively, Tertullian's admission that the story circulated orally as a "holy story" (or *hieros logos*) for women's ministries, the saturation of folkloric themes, the memory of Queen Tryphaena, and the popularity of Thecla in spite of the limited acceptance of the *Acts of Paul*—all suggest that the Asian presbyter borrowed the story from an old but still vital oral tradition. I know of no one who agrees with Tertullian's charge that the author created the story from scratch.

THE EPHESUS STORY

The Ephesus story is a Christian version of "Androcles [or, more correctly, Androclus] and the Lion." Androclus, a Roman slave, fled into a northern African wilderness to escape his cruel master who was serving as proconsul there. While he was hiding in a cave, a lion approached limping on a wounded paw. Instead of devouring the intruder of his lair, the lion offered his paw, from which Androclus removed a large splinter and drained the pus. The two became intimate companions, and even shared the cave for three years. Weary of this speluncar home, Androclus returned to the city. He was arrested and condemned to the beasts. The beast that was released against him was the very lion he had formerly befriended. When the lion licked Androclus' feet, the spectators were so moved they released the lion and Androclus.

The story appears in the *Attic Nights* of Aulus Gellius (5.14; ca. 160 C.E.). Gellius borrowed it from Apion's *Aegyptiaca* (first century C.E.), but no doubt the story originated in oral tradition. At the theater in Corinth archaeologists have discovered at the bottom of a wall enclosing the orchestra a series of paintings of human figures fighting with wild animals, under one of which is an inscription reading: "The lion recognizes the man under the bull as his savior and licks him."[29] Since the orchestra wall dates from early in the first century C.E., the tale apparently was popular lore by that time.

In the *Acts of Paul,* Paul tells the Ephesians that once he had been accosted by a ferocious lion, who, on hearing him preach, believed and was baptized. As a result of Paul's story about the lion, so many attached themselves to the apostle that the jaundiced authorities condemned him to be eaten by a recently captured lion. Of course, the lion was none other than the one Paul had baptized, and Paul was spared. Embedded in this larger story is another that is also full of traditional themes, such as a miraculous prison escape, a persecution by a jealous husband, ghosts, and the restoration of the dead to life.

Furthermore, we have good evidence that this story was known in the early church apart from the *Acts of Paul.* Hippolytus of Rome wrote in his *Commentary on Daniel* (ca. 202): "For if we believe that when Paul was condemned to beasts, the lion let loose on him fell at his feet and licked him, how shall we not believe the things that happened to Daniel?"[30] Hippolytus not only indicates here that those in his community ("we") believed this story about Paul, he even uses their belief in it to lend credibility to the Daniel story. Several scholars have seen evidence here that the *Acts of Paul* was used widely in Rome at the beginning of the third century,[31] but this judgment would seem quite unjustified. Apart from this one passage, there is absolutely no evidence that the *Acts of Paul* was known in Rome or anywhere else in the West before Ambrose late in the fourth century.[32] It is much more likely that the Romans knew of this story through oral tradition.

In one passage of Ignatius' letter to the Romans (ca. 107) we find evidence that Ignatius also had heard of beasts who had refused to eat those thrown to them:

> I long for the beasts that are prepared for me; and I pray that
> they may be found prompt for me; I will even entice them to
> devour me promptly; not as has happened to some whom
> they have not touched from fear.[33]

There is no story about reluctant wild beasts in Christian narratives that
were written before Ignatius. Of course, he might have been referring to
Jewish or Greek stories and persons such as Daniel and Dionysus. But if
he was referring to stories about previous Christians—as I would judge
to be most likely—he probably knew the stories from oral sources, and
the story about Paul and the Ephesian lion can claim more antiquity than
any other.

The author of the Pastoral Epistles also knew the Ephesian lion story.
In 2 Timothy, Paul tells the young bishop of Ephesus that all had
previously abandoned him, and that the Lord had stood by him, "that all
the Gentiles might hear" his message. Even though these Gentiles did
not accept Paul's message but condemned him to the beasts, God spared
his life: "So I was rescued from the lion's mouth" (2 Tim. 4:16–17).
These verses are remarkably consistent with the version of the legend
which appears in the *Acts of Paul* where all abandon Paul in Ephesus,
Paul gives his solo defense before the Gentiles, is sentenced to be eaten
by a lion, and ultimately is spared. In Chapter III we shall see that this is
but one piece of evidence indicating that the author of the Pastoral
Epistles knew the legends behind the *Acts of Paul.*

In a recent article I argued from an analysis of 1 Cor. 15:32 that Paul
himself knew and disapproved of this story: "What do I gain if, humanly
speaking, I fought with beasts at Ephesus?" I shall not encumber the
present discussion by repeating the argument here, since those interested can easily find it,[34] and since the traditionality of the legend can be
established apart from this interpretation of 1 Cor. 15:32. The popularity of the Androclus and the Lion tale type and the references in
Hippolytus, Ignatius, and the Pastoral Epistles are sufficient to suggest
that, as with the Thecla story, the author of the *Acts of Paul* borrowed this
story from an oral tradition which reached back into the first half of the
second century—and perhaps back to Paul's time as well.

THE MARTYRDOM STORY

Like the previous two stories, the story of Paul's martyrdom in Rome is
full of folkloric themes, such as a theophanic *quo vadis?* scene, a
resuscitation of a corpse, an imperial trial, and appearances of Paul's
ghost. No doubt stories of Paul's death were told far and wide. The
author of the Acts of the Apostles, Clement of Rome, and Ignatius all

knew of them,[35] but apart from saying that Paul was beheaded in Rome during the reign of Nero they give no information concerning their content. Consequently, we cannot use them to establish how much of the story in the *Acts of Paul* might have been traditional. But there is some evidence suggesting that at least one element of the story was known long before the writing of the *Acts of Paul*.

Eusebius says that the daughters of Philip told Papias about a certain Barsabas Justus who was forced to drink poison and was miraculously saved from its effects.[36] Eusebius recognized that the Acts of the Apostles also mentions a Barsabas Justus: he was one of the two followers of Jesus eligible to replace Judas among the Twelve (Acts 1:23). But it is highly unusual for a Christian to have been given poison as a means of execution. In fact, I have found no other example of poison used for this purpose in any ante-Nicean source.[37] Poison was reserved for Roman officials or soldiers accused of treason. I suggest that the story told by the daughters of Philip was not about the Barsabas Justus in Acts but about another man with the same name who, according to the *Acts of Paul,* was in fact a Roman soldier who was saved from execution.

In the *Acts of Paul,* Paul is brought before Nero for judgment, and during the hearing several of Nero's own military guard—including one named Barsabas Justus—admit to being soldiers of Paul's King. Nero orders these traitors executed along with the other Christians, but when the Romans complain about the many deaths of their fellow citizens Nero relents. Barsabas Justus and his friends are released. We are not told in the *Acts of Paul* by what good fortune Barsabas was spared while so many others were killed. At this point, of course, the story known to the daughters of Philip would fit perfectly: Barsabas was ordered to drink poison and was unaffected. It appears that the Barsabas Justus story told by the daughters of Philip was one episode in a legend about Paul's death, but for some reason was omitted, except for a trace, in the *Acts of Paul.* If we are correct in linking the two stories, at least one episode of the martyrdom story in the *Acts of Paul* was known several decades before the *Acts of Paul* was written. Perhaps the longer ending of Mark also reflects a knowledge of this story, for here the risen Christ promises his followers that "if they drink any deadly thing, it will not hurt them" (Mark 16:18). This ending to the Gospel was already known to Justin Martyr and Tatian, and therefore must have been written before the second half of the second century.

The reference to Barsabas Justus is also important for illustrating the method of composition used in the *Acts of Paul.* The author obviously was not obsessed with squaring his accounts with those in the Acts of the

Apostles or the biographical references in Paul's letters. In addition to the *Acts of Paul* shipping Barsabas Justus, the Palestinian Jew, off to Rome and dressing him in Roman arms, there are several other blatant discrepancies between the *Acts of Paul* and the New Testament. These discrepancies require some explaining, since the author undoubtedly knew some of the Gospels, some of Paul's letters, and probably also the Acts of the Apostles.[38] The interpreter is forced to judge between two options. Either the author was a presumptuous fabricator, who, although knowing some of the New Testament writings, freely differed from them when it pleased his fancy; or he received his stories independently from a legendary tradition which he highly respected, and used rather innocently without harmonizing the stories with Acts or the Epistles. I agree with Wilhelm Schneemelcher in preferring the second option.

> The author of the AP adhered to Acts neither in the matter of the route nor in respect of other facts. He collected and arranged his material independently. In so doing he certainly to a great extent followed a current legendary tradition.[39]

For example, in the canonical book of Acts, Paul is arrested in Jerusalem, then is taken to Rome, where he freely teaches while awaiting execution. But in the *Acts of Paul* the arrest takes place in Rome, and soon afterward he is beheaded. Of course, it is possible that the author, like Clement of Rome and the author of the *Acts of Peter,* thought Paul had been released from his first imprisonment, gone to Spain (as he had hoped, Rom. 15:24 and 28), and later was again arrested, tried, and executed. But the *Acts of Paul* says nothing about a visit to Spain; Paul arrives in Rome for the last time, coming from the east. It would appear that here we have a variant tradition of Paul's execution which differed from both the Acts account and the Spain tradition. Furthermore, even though the *Acts of Paul* contains stories about cities in the Pauline mission (the Antioch of Syria and of Pisidia, Iconium, Lystra, Ephesus, Corinth, Rome, and others), the contents of the stories in the *Acts of Paul* share almost nothing with references to the same cities in the Epistles or Acts.

The martyrdom story in the *Acts of Paul* also contains a story similar to that in Acts 20:9–12 about Eutychus, who, while listening to Paul preach, falls from a window, dies, and is raised again. But in the *Acts of Paul* the perilously perched youth is Patroclus, Nero's cupbearer. Patroclus comes to the barn where Paul is preaching, and because of the crowd he is forced to sit in a high window, from which he falls and dies. To the astonishment of all present, Paul restores him to life. It is possible, of course, that the author knew of the story from Acts and substituted Patroclus' name for Eutychus, but it is also possible that both he and the author of Acts knew of the story from oral tradition. Only our Western prejudice for written dependence would make us think the author picked this story out of a book and not out of the tale-rich air.

THE ORAL FORM OF THE STORIES

Thus far we have shown that the author of the *Acts of Paul* did not create our three stories *ex nihilo* but took them over from popular legend tradition. However, it remains to be seen how much of the stories in their present form may have come from the tradition and how much from the hand of the author. That is, although he seems to have borrowed traditional stories, he may have recast them into a form quite unlike any they had orally. One thinks of how Aeschylus used and altered Orestes legends in his play, how Goethe used Faust legends in his romantic poem, and how Alex Haley used Kunta Kinte legends in his historical novel. But even in their present written versions our three stories adhere to conventions of oral narrative as defined by folklorists. It would appear, therefore, that the written text of the stories is a veneer laid over narrative structures and techniques taken over from oral tradition.

One of the most successful attempts to distinguish between the conventions of oral and written narratives is that of Alex Olrik, who epitomized his results in an article entitled "Epic Laws of Folk Narrative."[40] Before we apply his analysis to the stories, however, I should offer a word of caution, in that Olrik believes he has found in folk narrative abstract principles that control the transmission of the folk story. Other folklorists rejected such "superorganic" approaches, arguing that they "take the folk out of folklore."[41] The rigidity of Olrik's "laws" suggests that the storyteller is merely the medium through which the story type generates another story, something like suggesting that a chicken is merely the medium through which an egg creates another egg.

Olrik's article, however, is still quoted and used as a classic even by folklorists who have replaced his superorganic model with a more sophisticated and flexible one supplied by generative linguistics. This new model appreciates storytellers as artists creating within the canons of their medium, and not as passive transmitters of narrative structures with interchangeable content. According to folklorists who use this further generative linguistic approach, stories, like sentences, have syntactic structures that hold them together and allow for meaningful decoding. For example, anyone who speaks French has internalized the syntactic patterns of French, patterns which in no way dictate the content of a sentence but nonetheless are absolutely essential for constructing a sentence meaningfully. One could call these patterns "laws," providing one understood them to be like rules for chess which allow players to exchange pieces in an orderly way but do not decide the outcome of the game. So too with stories: storytellers have internalized traditional ethnopoetic canons or rules of composition that characterize a storytelling tradition. These canons help the storyteller to shape experiences into meaningful stories, to tell coherent stories that last for several evenings, to remember hundreds of such stories, and even to learn an epic poem at only one hearing.[42] Therefore, we can still use Olrik's laws if we understand them not as impersonal, abstract, inviolable laws but as observable canons used by storytellers to assist them in the tale-telling process. These laws also sometimes appear in written stories. While it is impossible to use these laws—or any others—as a fool-proof litmus test for orality, we *can* show that our stories contain characteristics almost always found in oral narratives and often absent in written ones.

THE LAW OF OPENING

Olrik observed that oral narrative never begins with sudden action; rather, it "begins by moving from calm to excitement."[43] All three of our stories begin calmly by having Paul travel from one city to another where he is welcomed by local believers. Later, people in the city hostile to the Christian cause take him or Thecla before the authorities, who then condemn them to die. Only after this do the stories rise to their peaks of intensity when God rescues the protagonist from the execution attempt, or, in the case of the martyrdom story, when the execution attempt is successful. Each story gradually and steadily proceeds from hospitality to hostility and ultimately to divine intervention.

THE LAW OF CONCENTRATION ON A LEADING CHARACTER

According to Olrik, "the greatest law of folk tradition is *Concentration on a Leading Character*."[44] This law applies beautifully to the Ephesus and martyrdom stories, where Paul clearly is the protagonist throughout. The Thecla story, however, seems to violate this principle, for it begins by concentrating on Paul but soon changes to Thecla, who remains the protagonist until the end. But Olrik's law also accounts for this apparent variation.

> It is very interesting to see how folk narrative proceeds when the *Sage* [by which Olrik means all genres of oral narrative] recognizes two heroes. One is always the formal protagonist.

The *Sage* begins with his story and from all outward appearances he is the principal character. The king's son, not the monster's daughter is the formal protagonist of the folktale about the forgotten fiancée.... When a man and woman appear together, the man is the most important character. Nevertheless, the actual interest frequently lies with the woman. It is the forgotten fiancée and not the king's son for whom we have the greater sympathy.[45]

This change in protagonists is exactly what we find in the Thecla story.

THE LAW OF CONTRAST

Even though oral narrative concentrates on a leading character, its development requires a conflict between the hero and at least one foe. This feature Olrik labels *"The Law of Contrast,"* which characteristically "works from the protagonist of the *Sage* out to the other individuals, whose characteristics and actions are determined by the requirement that they be antithetical to those of the protagonist."[46] Where there is no conflict, there is no story. "The *Sage* is always polarized."[47]

Each of our stories begins with descriptions of Paul's virtues, and thereafter all other characters find their place in relationship to him. Paul and Thamyris, rivals for Thecla's heart, represent respectively goodness-chastity-sobriety and their opposite, wickedness-lust-drunkenness. Onesiphorus hosts Paul, while Demas and Hermogenes betray him. Theocleia, Thecla's unbelieving and hostile mother, is placed over against Tryphaena, Thecla's believing and hospitable second mother. The women and the lioness befriend Thecla against the wiles of the men and the lion. In the Ephesus story too, Ammia's household turns against Paul, but Procla's household turns toward him. Diophantes and Hieronymus oppose their wives Eubula and Artemilla, who have gone after Paul. Again, in the martyrdom story Paul and his companions, Titus and Luke, are pitted against Nero and his companions, Longus and Cestus. So complete is the polarization of characters that no one appears unaligned with one of the opposing camps. Those not for Paul are viciously against him.

THE LAW OF TWINS

Olrik noticed that some people in oral narrative "can evade the Law of Contrast and become subjugated instead to the *Law of Twins.* ... Beings of subordinate rank appear in duplicate: two Dioscuri are messengers of Zeus; two ravens or two Valkyries, messengers of Odin."[48] In other words, frequently two minor characters appear with no individual distinguishing features, like Cinderella's two jealous stepsisters. We find this convention of oral narrative over and over again in our stories.

In the Thecla story Paul's two fellow travelers, Demas and Hermogenes, possess no individual qualities. In fact, three times we find "Demas and Hermogenes said," as if they were speaking in unison. Likewise, Onesiphorus' two sons, Simmias and Zeno, together say to Paul: "We are hungry," and Paul sends one of them—we are not told which one, nor does it matter—to buy bread. In the Ephesus story Paul stays with Aquila and Priscilla, tells his story about walking in Phoenicia with Lemma and Ammia, and afterward he converts Artemilla and Eubula. In the martyrdom story Cleobius and Myrta prophesy Paul's death, Luke and Titus await Paul in Rome, Nero's men Parthenius and Pheretas go to see if Paul had been executed, and the officials Longus and Cestus are converted by Titus and Luke. Notice how these last two sets of twins function in the following excerpt. Not one of the four characters has qualities distinguishing him from his twin.

> As Paul directed, Longus and Cestus went at dawn and with fear approached Paul's tomb. But as they drew near they saw two men praying, and Paul between them, so that at the sight of this unexpected wonder they were astounded, while Titus and Luke were seized with human fear when they saw Longus and Cestus coming towards them, and turned to flight. But they followed after them, saying: "We are not pursuing you to kill you, as you imagine, ye blessed men of God, but for life, that you may give it to us as Paul promised us, whom we saw but now standing between you and praying." And when Titus and Luke heard this from them, with great joy they gave them the seal in the Lord.[49]

THE LAW OF THE SINGLE STRAND

According to Olrik, "folk narrative is always *single-stranded,*" in contrast to the complex, entangled plots often encountered in written stories. When the oral narrator must provide background information, "it will be given in dialogue. In the city, the hero of the tale hears of the man-eating dragon who has caused misery throughout the land. Siegfried hears the story of the Rhinegold from Regin."[50]

The plots of our stories are simple, economical, and single-stranded. Each moves forward chronologically toward its resolution. There are, however, back references to supply necessary information from the past, and they are given in dialogue, just as Olrik observed elsewhere. The clearest example of this back-referencing appears in the Ephesus story, where Paul in a sermon tells of his baptizing a lion in Phoenicia. By means of this device the storyteller can break the sequence momentarily

to splice in a picture from the past in order to let the hearer/reader see
the background conditions that are necessary for the rest of the story.
Notice also that this same device appears in the Androclus story,
according to Aulus Gellius. It begins with Androclus in the Great Circus
about to be eaten by wild beasts when a lion runs up to him and licks his
feet and hands. The emperor summons Androclus and asks him why the
lion refused to eat him. When Androclus tells that he had healed the
lion's paw and shared his cave, the emperor releases both man and beast.
The presence of this back-referencing device in both stories suggests
that the device itself was traditional. As George Bernard Shaw recognized while writing his play *Androcles and the Lion* (in which Androcles is a
Christian!), a more logical development of the story would begin with
the removal of the splinter from the lion's paw and proceed to the scene
in the arena.

Apart from such back references,[51] our stories move on toward their
resolution with little deviation from their single strand.

THE LAW OF REPETITION

Perhaps no convention of oral narrative is more universal than
repetition. The pauper wins three contests in order to marry the
princess; Jack steals three objects from the heavenly giant; Little Red
Riding Hood asks four questions of the wolf in disguise; the poor wise
maiden must solve four riddles; during several consecutive nights the
miller's daughter spins gold for the king with the help of Rumpelstilts-
kin, who gives her three chances to guess his name. According to Olrik:

> Every time that a striking scene occurs in a narrative, and
> continuity permits, the scene is repeated. This is necessary
> not only to build tension, but to fill out the body of the
> narrative. There is intensifying repetition and simple repeti-
> tion, but the important point is that without repetition, the
> *Sage* cannot attain its fullest form.[52]

Our stories certainly are no exception to the rule. The Thecla story is a
duplication of scenarios, one taking place at Iconium, the other at
Antioch. In both, Thecla's frustrated lover secures her death sentence
from the local Roman authority, but she is miraculously rescued and
leaves the city to look for Paul. Within the second of these two
symmetrical stories we find four attempts to kill Thecla: When the
authorities release lions and bears against her, a lioness kills them; when
Thecla throws herself into a pool of vicious seals, lightning kills them;
when they send in other beasts, the women spectators drug them to sleep

by throwing spices and perfumes into the arena; finally, when her legs are tied to two bulls, a fire burns the ropes.

In the martyrdom story, in order to emphasize that Paul's death was providential, the storyteller says that the Holy Spirit came on three prophets—Paul, Cleobius, and Myrta—who sequentially forecast different aspects of the apostle's fate. As though the threefold forecast were not enough, Paul prophesies again the following morning.

THE USE OF TABLEAUX SCENES

Olrik observed that oral narratives always rise to peaks in the form of "tableaux scenes," about which he wrote:

> These sculptured situations are based more on fantasy than on reality: the hero's sword is scorched by the dragon's breath; the maiden, standing on the back of a bull or a snake, surveys the scene; from her own breasts the banished queen squeezes milk into the beaks of a swan and a crane.[53]

In our stories as well, reality gives way to fantasy as each story rises to its peak in the vindication of the protagonist at the moment of execution. The first of these four scenes appears in the Iconium section of the Thecla story where she is brought into the theater naked, mounts the pyre, and stretches out her arms, making the sign of the cross. Miraculously, the flames cannot harm her, for rain and hail extinguish them and disperse the crowd. The second "tableau scene" comes at the end of Thecla's visit to Antioch, where she is stripped, thrown into the stadium, and exposed to wild beasts none of whom is able to harm her. The third such scene consists of Paul in the Ephesian arena facing the baptized lion who comes and licks the apostle. When the governor sends in more beasts and archers, hail falls, killing or scattering the spectators. The fourth and last example appears in the martyrdom story where Paul is taken before the executioner, prays in Hebrew facing east, and bares his neck. Milk spurts from Paul's severed neck and all are amazed. Clearly, each of these scenes is "based more on fantasy than on reality." Furthermore, one can illustrate the picturesque or tableau nature of these narrative sections by referring to the iconography of Paul and Thecla in which the apostle is shown with a lion or about to be beheaded, and Thecla shown surrounded by wolves, snakes, lion, or fire.[54]

THE LAW OF CLOSING

> After the concluding event, in which the principle character frequently has a catastrophe, the *Sage* ends by moving from excitement to calm. . . . The constant reappearance of this

element of terminal calm shows that it is based, not just on a manifestation of the inclination of an individual narrator, but on the formal constraint of an epic law.[55]

None of our stories end with the tableau scene; each has a denouement or epilogue which lowers the intensity of the peak and brings the story to terminal calm. These denouements put the major characters of the story to rest by indicating their reactions to the protagonist's fate. For example, at the end of the Thecla story we find the responses of Tryphaena and her maidservants, of Theocleia, and of Christians in Seleucia. The martyrdom story ends with Nero's change of heart at seeing Paul alive and with the conversions of Longus and Cestus. Even though the text of the Ephesus story is extremely fragmentary at the end, we know, thanks to an epitome of Nicephorus Callistus (*Church History* 2, 25, fourteenth century), that the epilogue told of the conversion of Hieronymus, the Roman governor.[56]

NARRATIVE INCONSISTENCIES

The last convention of oral narratives that we shall apply to the stories is borrowed, not from Olrik, but from another folklorist. In his analysis of Yugoslav epic poems Albert B. Lord has observed "occasional inconsistency, the famous nod of a Homer," which he claims is "that characteristic of oral poetry which literary scholars have found hardest to understand and to accept."[57] Such inconsistencies are not restricted to oral poetry; they appear in all genres of oral narrative, but they are relatively uncommon in written narrative. The reason is clear. Because writers can reread their stories after they have written them, they can more easily detect inconsistencies and make the necessary adjustments. Storytellers cannot.

Inconsistencies abound in our stories. In the Ephesus story, Paul tells of being entertained in Phoenicia by the widow Lemma and her daughter Ammia. Just after this speech is finished, the story again speaks of Ammia, but now she is no longer a companion of Paul in Phoenicia but a resident of Ephesus who turns against him. In the martyrdom story, when Paul is brought to the imperial court he preaches to Nero and then to his lieutenants, Longus and Cestus. While narrating these speeches, the storyteller apparently forgets that the scene is in Nero's court, because immediately afterward we find: "Nero sent a certain Parthenius and Pheretas to see if Paul had already been beheaded," as if Paul were in jail or on the executioner's stand. Similarly, the Thecla story contains duplications of elements which suggest that the storyteller accidentally jumped ahead of the story or otherwise skewed the progression and had to back up and repeat parts of the story. In the following passage, notice that Thecla throws herself into the water twice:

> And when she had finished her prayer, she turned and saw a great pit full of water, and said: "Now is the time for me to wash." And SHE THREW HERSELF IN, saying: "*In the name of Jesus Christ* I baptize myself on the last day!" And when they saw it, the women and all the people wept, saying: "Cast not thyself into the water!"; so that even the governor wept that such beauty should be devoured by seals. So, then, SHE THREW HERSELF INTO THE WATER *in the name of Jesus Christ.* (AP 3:34; emphasis added)

These are some of the more blatant inconsistencies; there are several others. Again, such loose narrative constructions are not definitive proof of orality, but they are more frequent and less noticeable in oral stories than in written ones.

If our arguments in this chapter have been correct, it would appear that the second-century Asian presbyter who wrote the *Acts of Paul* appropriated these three legends from oral tradition. The orality of the legends can be demonstrated both from their characteristically folkloric content and from their conformity to the conventions of oral narratives. These observations are confirmed by external evidence that each of them was known apart from the *Acts of Paul.*

CHAPTER II

The Storytellers
Behind the Legends

The existence of oral antecedents to the stories in the *Acts of Paul* allows us to pursue investigations that would be impossible if the stories had been created exclusively at the time they were written. Oral narrative is a social phenomenon unlike most written narrative. If stories are to thrive orally, they must have active channels for transmission (i.e., storytellers) as well as passive channels (sympathetic audiences). When folklorists study oral narrative they seldom limit themselves to the analysis of formal features, as we did in the preceding chapter. Instead, they ask: Who told the stories? To whom were they told? When, where, and why were they told? The three stories we have studied also disclose much about their origins. In this chapter we shall see that those who told the stories probably were celibate women in Asia Minor who expected Christ soon to destroy the world and to rescue the righteous. This apocalypticism was attended by contempt for Asia Minor social institutions, especially the household. In Chapter III, I shall suggest that the author of the Pastoral Epistles, knowing these "old wives' tales" and incensed by their use of Paul's memory to sanction socially radical sectarianism, put his hand to the quill in order to depict a more domestic, quiescent, and respectable Paul.

THE GENDER OF THE STORYTELLERS

Even though Tertullian's testimony to the *Acts of Paul* says the author was a male presbyter, the legends display a sensitivity to the concerns of women that is extremely rare in early Christian writings. This "women's point of view" has so impressed one scholar that he has rejected Tertullian's testimony as a polemical fabrication and has argued that the author of the *Acts of Paul* actually was a woman.[1] But one need not make Tertullian a liar in order to account for the prominence of women's concerns in the legends. If we are correct in claiming that the author of the *Acts of Paul* took these legends from oral tradition, the sensitivity to women might well be attributed to female storytellers. In fact, we have strong external and internal evidence suggesting that women did indeed tell these stories.

Tertullian knew that some people told the story of Thecla in order to legitimate women teaching and baptizing. He does not indicate whether women themselves told the story, but it is reasonable to think they did. It is clear that other women in the early church cited holy women of the past as precedents to justify their ministries. The Montanist prophetesses Maximilla and Priscilla legitimated their ministries by citing precedents in Ammia of Philadelphia and the daughters of Philip.[2] Likewise, Quintillian female clergy appealed to the examples of the daughters of Philip, of Miriam, Moses' prophesying sister, and even of Eve, since she was the first person to eat of the tree of knowledge.[3]

Once again, the comparison of this story with the story about Hagnodice is instructive: just as Thecla legitimated women teachers, Hagnodice legitimated women physicians. Because the story of Hagnodice displays hostility for men and sympathy for women, especially in childbearing, it would seem reasonable to think that women themselves told it.

If the author of the *Acts of Paul* did in fact write down the oral communications of women, he was not the first or the last early Christian author to do so. Papias, bishop of Hierapolis, Phrygia, early in the second century incorporated into his *Expositions of the Oracles of the Lord* at least two stories he had heard from the daughters of Philip the evangelist (cf. Acts 21:7–9).[4] The Marcionite Apelles wrote a book consisting of the oracles of the prophetess Philoumene,[5] and the Montanist Asterius Urbanus wrote down the oracles of the prophetess Maximilla.[6] It is quite likely that the books of Maximilla and Priscilla known to Theodoret and Didymus the Blind were not actually written by the women themselves but by their followers.[7]

Evidence internal to our three stories also points to female storytellers. In the Thecla story, we are told that those who come to hear Paul preach are "women and the young," or "women and virgins" like Thecla. The Iconians complain that Paul beguiled their wives. Thecla's mother asks the governor to burn her, so "that all the women who have been taught by this man may be afraid." Notice also the significance of women in the following précis of one episode:

> In Antioch of Pisidia Thecla defended herself against the
> violent embraces of Alexander, whom the local governor

appeased by condemning Thecla to the beasts, in spite of the protests of Antiochean women. When Thecla asked to be kept pure from men until the day of her execution, she was entrusted to Queen Tryphaena, and was escorted to her home by crying women. While with Tryphaena, Thecla offered a prayer for the widow's deceased daughter. Although Tryphaena and the other women again protested the injustice, the soldiers finally took Thecla to the theater, where they released wild beasts against her. Then a "fierce lioness ran to her and lay down at her feet. And the crowd of women raised a great shout." A bear ran against Thecla and the lioness killed it. When a lion was released, the lioness fought with it until both died. "And the women mourned the more, since the lioness which helped her was dead." When the men released more beasts, "the women threw petals, others nard, others cassia, others amomum, so that there was an abundance of perfumes. And all the beasts let loose were overpowered as if by sleep." Then the men tied Thecla's feet to two bulls and placed red-hot irons on their genitals. But when the bulls leapt forward the ropes were burned. At this Tryphaena fainted. Thinking she had died and fearing imperial reprisals for the death of this member of the royal family, the authorities released Thecla to her cheering sisters. Tryphaena, revived, received Thecla once again into her house, and the majority of her maidservants converted to Christ.[8]

The significance of this episode is not merely that women predominate. Like the story of Hagnodice, it treats all women sympathetically and all men contemptuously. As one scholar has put it, the story reveals the perspective of "someone deeply resentful of the male sex and highly sensitive to the difficulties of women."[9] Not one male—man or beast, pagan or even apostolic—befriends Thecla. If the contents of any early Christian story suggests that its tellers were women, it is this one.

Likewise, the Ephesus story is dominated by female characters. Paul's travel companions are the widow Lemma and her daughter Ammia. Paul stays at the house of Aquila and Priscilla, but the household of Ammia turns against Paul because he had converted Procla and her household. While in prison, Paul converts Eubula and Artemilla, whose husbands are livid with jealousy because of their wives' love of Paul. The apostle's only male allies are Aquila, an angel, and a lion.

With regard to the martyrdom story we have direct linkage to women storytellers, if the Barsabas Justus mentioned there is the same Barsabas Justus about whom the daughters of Philip told their story to Papias.[10] They also told a story about how a woman, "the mother of Manaemus," was raised from death.[11] According to Eusebius, Papias knew of "another story about a woman who was accused before the Lord of many sins, which the Gospel according to the Hebrews contains."[12] Presumably, this is the story of the adulterous woman which appears in some texts of the Gospel of John between 7:52 and 8:12, and in which Jesus defends a woman against her male accusers. Papias knew the story only in its oral form, and quite possibly heard it from the daughters of Philip. In any case, the common reference to Barsabas Justus links celibate, female storytellers with legends that give prominence to just such celibate women. But even if such a coincidence were merely accidental, it would still seem likely that our stories were indeed "old wives' tales."

THE LOCATION OF THE STORYTELLERS

Undoutedly, those who told the stories lived somewhere in Asia Minor. The most obvious reason for locating them there is Tertullian's statement that the *Acts of Paul* was written by a presbyter in Asia. The reference to Queen Tryphaena of Pontus in the Thecla story also suggests this. But probably we should narrow our focus to south central Asia Minor: Phrygia, Pisidia, southern Galatia, and western Cappadocia. The Thecla story takes place in Iconium, Antioch, and Myra, and contains accurate references to local geography.[13] There are no such references in the stories narrating events in Ephesus or Rome. In fact, the martyrdom story evinces some Anatolian pride by identifying one of Nero's bodyguards as a Cappadocian (Urion) and another as a Galatian (Festus)—the only provincials mentioned in the story apart from Paul himself. These data correspond with the telling of the Barsabas Justus story in Hierapolis of Phrygia by the daughters of Philip. As late as the sixth century, Christians in south central Asia Minor venerated Thecla as a local saint.

Further confirmation of the Anatolian origin of the legends is the correspondence between the significant ecclesiastical functions of women in the legends and their actual functions in Asia Minor churches. As far as we can tell, women exercised more leadership on that subcontinent than anywhere else in the early church. If, as many scholars have suggested, the last chapter of Romans originally was Paul's letter of recommendation to Ephesus on behalf of the deacon Phoebe,[14] the Ephesian church not only hosted this female traveling deacon but had among its members a female apostle (Junia; Rom. 16:7), several female church workers (Priscilla, Mary, Tryphaena, Tryphosa, and Persis; vs. 3, 6, and 12), and other women dear to the apostle (the mother of Rufus, the sister of Nereus, and Julia; vs. 13, 15). But even if Romans 16 was not originally written to Ephesus, we still have ample evidence of women in leadership in Asia Minor. Priscilla and Aquila housed a church in Ephesus,[15] Apphia and Philemon in Colossae or the vicinity,[16] Nympha in Laodicea.[17] John the Seer scolded the church at Thyatira for having tolerated "that Jezebel, the woman who calls herself a prophetess, whose teaching misleads," and who had a sizable following (Rev. 2:18–25). The letter known as 2 John, probably written to Asia Minor, is addressed to "the elect lady and her children," who are greeted at the end of the letter by "the children" of her "elect sister." Unfortunately, it is impossible to know with certainty whether these "elect ladies" are simply ciphers for sister churches or whether they were real women. If real women, they were responsible for the nurture of other believers and for discerning which traveling teachers to admit into their homes (2 John, v. 10). In any case, Raymond E. Brown has shown that women enjoyed considerable respect in Johannine circles.[18]

Evidence of women in ecclesiastical leadership in Asia Minor is also apparent outside the New Testament. According to two second-century sources, the prophesying daughters of Philip mentioned in Acts 21:9 in connection with Caesarea moved to Hierapolis, where they continued their ministries.[19] Miltiades (ca. 160) wrote about the influence of Ammia of Philadelphia, whom he listed among "those who prophesied in the New Testament period."[20] Alkē of Smyrna, a friend of Ignatius, forty years after Ignatius' death was still revered in both Smyrna and Philomelium.[21] Pliny the Younger (ca. 112) wrote to the emperor Trajan that he received his information about the rites of Christians in Bithynia from two slave women who were deaconesses (*ministrae*).[22] Furthermore, several Greek inscriptions in Asia Minor contain the names of deaconesses.[23]

The importance of women is most obvious in the fragmentary evidence available about the Montanist movement in Phrygia. Priscilla and Maximilla were among the most influential prophetesses in the movement, and utterances from these and other women were cherished as divine revelation. Agathonice, a Pergamene second-century martyr, appears in one document as a prophet.[24] Ephiphanius says that a prophetess named Quintilla established a sect in Pepuza, Phrygia, in which women were "bishops, presbyters, and the rest, as if there were no difference in nature. 'For in Christ Jesus there is no male and female.' "[25] And Firmilian, a bishop in Cappadocia (ca. 260), wrote about a woman there who baptized and performed the Eucharist and who perhaps was a member of a Montanist or Quintillian congregation.[26] The Gnostic teacher Marcus was exceedingly successful among Asia

Minor women. According to Irenaeus, he deluded them into thinking they were prophetesses.[27]

Further evidence of the influence of women in Christian Asia Minor is the respect given to women of the past, like Thecla. Epiphanius says that the Nicolaitans, mentioned in the Apocalypse of John in connection with Ephesus and Pergamum, valued a book of Norea, Noah's wife or daughter-in-law.[28] Even though Epiphanius is notoriously unreliable when he writes of heretics in his own day—not to mention those in the first century—we need not reject his testimony *prima facie*. Thanks to the manuscript discoveries at Nag Hammadi, we now possess two documents in which Norea is the revealer,[29] and in another we find references to "the First Book [or, Logos] of Noraia" that lists the feminine names of the archons.[30] Irenaeus, Tertullian, and Clement of Alexandria all called the Nicolaitans Gnostics, and now that we know of at least three Gnostic books in which Norea is the revealer, it would appear that the Nicolaitans might well have revered her memory.[31]

Be that as it may, Hippolytus says the Naassenes or Ophites in Phrygia claimed to have received their doctrines from Mariamne, the sister of Philip the apostle.[32] The references to her in the *Sophia of Jesus Christ*, which probably originated in Ophite circles,[33] imply that she received secret revelations from Christ. Apparently the author of the *Acts of Philip* wanted to snatch Mariamne away from these Gnostics and give her lodging in his own theological camp, for according to him she accompanied her brother to Hierapolis in order to *refute* the Ophites.

Like Thecla, many of the women who ministered in Asia Minor were celibate. Two of the daughters of Philip died as virgins in Hierapolis, and their sister in Ephesus also probably retained her virginity throughout life.[34] Priscilla and Maximilla deserted their husbands from the moment they received prophetic inspiration, and Priscilla thereafter was called a virgin.[35] Quintilla and the Quintillian clergy were probably celibate, for Epiphanius says their assemblies often commenced with a procession of "seven virgins dressed in white . . . carrying lamps, having come in to prophesy to the people," and who wept, "lamenting human life."[36] In many contemporary sources this lamentation for human life was attended by asceticism designed to break the chain of birth.[37]

Furthermore, we have evidence that early in the second century or even in the first, churches in Asia Minor subsidized the order of widows. In his letter to the Smyrneans (ca. 107), Ignatius shows clearly that the order flourished in that city, and that some women there had been admitted into the register of widows who had never married: "I greet the houses of my brothers with their wives and children, and the virgins who are called 'widows.' "[38] Notice that the widows are considered outside the household arrangement. Tertullian too knew of a teenage virgin whom an Asian bishop had enrolled with the widows, but, unlike Ignatius, he was appalled by it.[39] Perhaps we should interpret this virginity as a rebellion—conscious or unconscious—against male domination. Perhaps it symbolized not only moral purity but also independence, dedication to a calling, and criticism of conjugal society. Whatever the motivation for their celibacy, it is precisely among such women that our legends probably enjoyed their most active lives.

But the legends disclose even more about the storytellers than their gender, location, and marital state. In fact, they allow us to reconstruct much about the way they viewed their world.

THE SOCIAL WORLD OF THE STORYTELLERS

Perhaps no vehicle for the transmission of social values is more universally effective than the folk story in providing popular sanctions for religious, social, and political institutions.[40] Even seemingly innocent fairytales like Sleeping Beauty, Rapunzel, Cinderella, and Snow White powerfully transmit attitudes toward witches, kinship relations, romance, and the roles of the sexes.[41] Furthermore, as William Hugh Jansen has shown in his article on "The Esoteric-Exoteric Factor in Folklore," cultural subgroups characteristically use oral folk narrative to establish the boundaries between the ingroup and outsiders, between the esoteric and exoteric.[42] It is clear that each of our three stories establishes boundaries between the church, epitomized by the protagonist, and the surrounding dominant and hostile society. By looking at the stories with an eye for these boundaries we can learn much about the social world of those who transmitted them.

OPPOSITION TO THE ROMAN EMPIRE

Each of our stories presupposes a conflict between the Roman Empire, convinced of its own legitimacy, power, and permanence, and an apocalyptic sect awaiting the destruction of the world. This expectation of the end provided them with a rival political vision, spawned radical social behavior, and promised divine vindication for those presecuted in the struggle.

For example, the martyrdom story contains a confrontation between Paul and Nero in which the kingdom of God is placed in direct opposition to the empire. The choice is clear: one cannot worship both Christ and Caesar. When Patroclus, Nero's cupbearer, is raised back to life, he tells the emperor that "Christ Jesus, the king of the ages" who will destroy all kingdoms under heaven, had raised him. Patroclus, Barsabas

Justus, Urion, and Festus confess to Nero that they all are soldiers of this "king of the ages." Nero orders them executed and asks Paul how he dared "to come secretly into the empire of the Romans and enlist soldiers." Paul answers that he enlists soldiers for his king from the whole world. If Nero does not repent, he will perish when Christ destroys the world with fire.

Perhaps the most interesting conflict between the idealized believer and the Roman state appears in Thecla's confrontation with Alexander in Antioch. From the description of Alexander it would appear that he was a Galatarch, an honorific local official responsible for financing—largely from his own purse—public banquets, games, and sacrifices, and for overseeing the imperial cult.[43] Apparently, on certain occasions Galatarchs wore gold wreaths bearing the emblem of the reigning emperor, as did the *stephanēphoroi* ("wreath bearers") in other Asian cities.[44]

According to our story, Alexander was a wealthy Syrian residing in Antioch of Pisidia who had been proclaimed "one of the first of the Antiochenes" (*AP* 3:26), presumably for his benefactions to the city.[45] He wore the wreath of the Galatarch and had arranged for a wild beast hunt and gladiatorial games. When he embraced Thecla on the street, she tore his *chlamys* (a mantle usually worn by imperial or military officials) and removed the wreath from his head, making him appear as one conquered *(thriambos)*. According to the Armenian version, Thecla "tore off the golden crown of the figure of Caesar, which he had on his head, and dashed it to the ground."[46] This variant, even if secondary, captures the intention of the original, for Alexander does not accuse her of assault but of sacrilege (*AP* 3:28). She had mocked the cult of the Augustus by violating the imperial numen associated with the wreath.

A similar sentiment against Rome and the imperial cult appears in the Apocalypse of John written to churches in western Asia Minor at the close of the first century. At least one Christian from the area had been martyred (Antipas of Pergamum, Rev. 2:13), and the author, himself an exile on Patmos, expected many more (see Rev. 6:9–11, and 20:4–6). Rome is depicted as a wanton harlot, her emperors are beasts, and all who cooperate with her will soon be punished at Christ's return (17:1–14; ch. 18). The faithful are summoned to separate themselves from her lest they too be punished for her sins (18:4–18), for they worship the King of Kings, who soon will establish his eternal kingdom (17:14; 20:1–10). As in the martyrdom story, the Apocalypse singles Nero out for particular contempt: he will return from the dead to battle Christ in the final war (17:7–14).[47] Notice also the similarity between the episode on Thecla's removing the imperial wreath from Alexander's head and statements in the Apocalypse about the mark of the beast which is invariably identified with emperor worship (13:15–18; 14:9–11; 19:20, 20:4). All those who wear the mark of the beast on their foreheads or right hands—i.e., wear wreaths or rings marked with imperial insignia?—will be thrown into the lake of fire (19:20), whereas those who refuse to wear the mark of the beast will forever wear the name of the Father on their foreheads (14:1; 20:4).[48] Clearly, the hostility toward the Roman Empire expressed in our legends was present in Asia Minor as early as the last decade of the first century.

OPPOSITION TO ASIA MINOR SOCIETY

In spite of this blatant hostility for Rome, the primary villains in the legends are not Romans but fellow Asians. The only Roman official who actively persecutes Christians is Nero; otherwise, these officials take measures against them only to placate local residents. Alexander, himself not a Roman but a Syrian and an honorary citizen of Antioch of Pisidia, brings charges against Thecla before the Roman governor, who is reluctant to execute her, later releases her, and calls her "the pious handmaid of God." Likewise in Iconium, a lynch mob seizes Paul, drags him before the governor, and demands his death. But the governor is not easily persuaded, hears Paul gladly, and releases him after a flogging. Only because Thecla's own mother requests the governor to execute her does he condemn her to the pyre. In the Ephesus story it is the Ephesians—especially the goldsmiths—who press charges against the apostle. The governor, though impressed by Paul's message, consents to his execution in order to quell a riot.

Once again it is clear that our legends reflect the actual state of affairs in Asia Minor from the beginning of the movement until the end of the second century. In about 55 C.E., Paul himself wrote that in Asia he and his companions "were so utterly, unbearably crushed that we despaired of life itself" (2 Cor. 1:8b). Unfortunately, he does not tell us whether the persecution was initiated by the local populace or by the Romans. However, about a year later Paul instructed Christians in Rome to obey the governing authorities, "for rulers are not a terror to good conduct, but to bad" (Rom. 13:3). Had the persecution in Asia been instigated by Roman political officials, it would be difficult to explain Paul's praise for them. Furthermore, according to the Acts of the Apostles, local residents drove Paul from Antioch of Pisidia (Acts 13:45–50), almost stoned him in Iconium (14:5), did in fact stone him in Lystra (14:19), and would have killed him in Ephesus (19:23–41). Even though we must be skeptical of the historical accuracy of these passages in Acts, the general depiction of popular resentment for Christians probably is correct.

Compare the claims of 1 John and Ignatius, both identified with Asia Minor, that the world hates Christians.[49] Surely we must not dismiss these statements as mere expressions of paranoia.

This popular animosity is also evident in Pliny's correspondence with Trajan. In a letter to the emperor, Pliny, a Roman administrator in Bithynia in 112, complains that the local temples were almost deserted because Christians were proselytizing from every level of society: young and old, men and women, urban and rural.[50] Their popularity among some, however, had sparked hatred in others who had circulated an anonymous list containing the names of alleged Christians. It is clear that Pliny himself harbored no animus for Christians; in fact, he knew little about them or their religion except that it had been outlawed. He executed some of them, but only because they were so unreasonably stubborn. It was not the Romans but the Bithynians themselves who had initiated the persecution.

The situation was essentially the same twelve years later in the province of Asia. The emperor Hadrian warned Minucius Fundanus, the Roman administrator there, not to yield too easily to "the rascality of informers" who were harassing the church.[51] Some Asians had used the official ban of Christianity for blackmail, but were unwilling to pursue the matter in court lest their accusations be judged groundless and therefore malicious. At about the same time the Asian Quadratus wrote an apology for the movement to Hadrian "because some wicked men were trying to trouble the Christians."[52]

The situation worsened by the year 177 when Melito of Sardis wrote the following complaint to Marcus Aurelius:

> It has never before happened as it is now that the race of the religious should be persecuted and driven about by new decrees throughout Asia. For shameless informers and lovers of other people's property have taken advantage of the decrees, and pillage us openly, harrying night and day those who have done nothing wrong. . . . And if this is done as your command, let it be assumed that it is well done, for no righteous king would ever have an unrighteous policy, and we gladly bear the honour of such death.[53]

But Melito was confident that the emperor wished to help the Christians, for he pled: "Do not neglect us in this brigandage by a mob."[54] In other words, even though Rome certainly had been no friend to the church, believers in Asia expected her to protect them from the criminal hostilities of their local adversaries. Under Aurelius, however, Rome either encouraged these acts of violence or winked at them.

Many factors contributed to this popular resentment. Greeks and Romans were generally tolerant of religions, providing they were not exclusive, like the Jews, or immoral, like the Bacchae. In the minds of some, Christians were guilty on both counts. Of course, they were evangelistically exclusive: their God and no other existed. Our stories include this exclusivity among the charges against Paul: Ephesian goldsmiths demanded his death for shrinking their market for religious *objets d'art*. He had "destroyed the gods of the Romans and the people." The charge of immorality consisted of rumors about Christian eucharistic cannibalism and Oedipal sex.[55]

Still others, like Pliny, complained of their fanaticism, which often extended to suicidal martyrdom. For example, Tertullian proudly informs us:

> When Arrius Antoninus was driving things hard in Asia [in Cappadocia, in 175], the whole Christians of the province, in one united band, presented themselves before his judgment-seat; on which, ordering a few to be led forth to execution, he said to the rest, "O miserable men, if you wish to die, you have precipes or halters."[56]

This eagerness to die apparently was encouraged by interpretations of the Apocalypse of John where it says that God will not avenge the blood of the martyrs until the full number of martyrs has been completed (Rev. 6:9–11). Furthermore, those who are "beheaded for their testimony to Jesus" will be raised in the first resurrection and reign as priests with Christ for a thousand years (20:4–6). This willingness to die was admired by some pagans—like Justin Martyr before his conversion—but in the eyes of many others, such as Arrius Antoninus, it was reprehensible and irrational masochism.

But the repulsion for Christians goes deeper than objections to their exclusivity, alleged immorality, or masochism; it is rooted in the hostility that societies often have for the marginality of apocalyptic groups.[57] One result of the claims by such groups that the world soon will be transformed by supernatural intervention is their reappraisal of conformity to dominant cultural expectations such as sexual mores, kinship relations, and economic obligations. Victor Turner's catalog of the radical characteristics of apocalyptic movements can be applied with few qualifications to the communities responsible for our legends:

> homogeneity, equality, anonymity, absence of property (many movements actually enjoin on their members the destruction of what property they possess to bring nearer the

coming of the perfect state of unison and communion they desire, for property rights are linked with structural distinctions both vertical and horizontal), reduction of all to the same status level, the wearing of uniform apparel (sometimes for both sexes), sexual continence (or its antithesis, sexual community, both continence and sexual community liquidate marriage and the family, which legitimate structural status), minimization of sex distinctions (all are "equal in the sight of God" or the ancestors), abolition of rank, humility, disregard for personal appearance, unselfishness, total obedience to the prophet or leader, sacred instruction, the maximization of religious, as opposed to secular, attitudes and behavior, suspension of kinship rights and obligations (all are siblings or comrades of one another regardless of previous secular ties), simplicity of speech and manners, sacred folly, acceptance of pain and suffering (even to the point of undergoing martyrdom), and so forth.[58]

That primitive Christianity possessed many of these properties Paul himself shows:

I mean, brethren, the appointed time has grown very short; from now on, let those who have wives live as though they had none, and those who mourn as though they were not mourning, and those who rejoice as though they were not rejoicing, and those who buy as though they had no goods, and those who deal with the world as though they had no dealings with it. For the form of this world is passing away. (1 Cor. 7:29–31)

Our legends faithfully preserve this aspect of Paul's teachings. For example, in his speech to Artemilla, Paul bids her to abandon her wealth inasmuch as God soon will destroy the world.[59] This impending destruction also dictates a reappraisal of sexuality. As Paul put it, "Let those who have wives live as though they had none" (1 Cor. 7:29). The beatitudes at the beginning of the Thecla story express the same sentiment:

Blessed are they who have renounced this world, for they shall be well pleasing unto God.
Blessed are they who have wives as if they had them not, for they shall inherit God . . . .
Blessed are they who through love of God have departed from the form of this world, for they shall judge angels and at the right hand of the Father they shall be blessed . . . .
Blessed are the bodies of the virgins, for they shall be well pleasing to God, and shall not lose the reward of their purity.

For the word of the Father shall be for them a work of
salvation in the day of his Son, and they shall have rest for
ever and ever. (*AP* 3:5–6)

In the following section I shall try to show that this renunciation of sex
and marriage, along with a general withdrawal from society, caused the
residents of Asia Minor to consider the church a rival to their most
treasured and central social institutions: the *polis*, or city, and the *oikia*, or
household. Of all the sources behind the popular resentment of Christians this was the *bête noire*.

OPPOSITION TO THE CITY AND THE HOUSEHOLD

Sometime between 161 and 165 a rhetorician in Smyrna named Aelius
Aristides lashed out against a local Cynic philosopher for flouting
generally accepted social conventions. While arguing against this Cynic,
he also attacked Christians and thereby tells us much about how the elite
in Asia Minor viewed them. He complains that they

> divide and upset the household *(oikia)*, and bring into colli-
> sion those inside with each other, and tell them the worst ways
> to manage their households. They never say, find, or do
> anything socially productive. They do not participate in
> panegyrics (festal assemblies for national gods), nor worship
> the gods, nor help govern the cities *(poleis)*, nor comfort the
> sorrowing, nor make reconciliation with those of opposing
> persuasions, nor arouse the young—or anyone else for that
> matter—to the affairs of the world.[60]

Not only does Aristides complain that Christians did not "participate
in panegyrics, nor worship the gods," he also complains that they shirk
public responsibility and upset the household. Apparently, his primary
objections to them are not to their religious practices, their theology, or
their attitudes toward the empire but to their social marginality, their
civic irresponsibility, and their domestic disruptiveness. Therefore, it is
no wonder that he denounces Christians in the context of denouncing
Cynics.

The word "cynic" means "doglike," a label these street philosophers
wore proudly. Their goal in life was "to live according to nature," by
which they meant to live according to the natural order of things and not
according to the conventions of human society. They claimed to be
"cosmopolitans"—that is, citizens of no one city—and wandered from
city to city preaching poverty, vilifying the status quo, insulting passers-
by, living from the beneficence of their followers, and fleeing from the
anger of their enemies. They eschewed marriage, civic commitments,

and social decency. Among their symbolic acts of defiance were urinating, defecating, and masturbating in public. Most Cynics were less extreme in their behavior,[61] but by self-definition they were socially marginal.

In spite of the obvious differences between Cynic preachers and Christian missionaries, there are many similarities. Both were indigent itinerants, and both preached a morality opposed to that of the dominant society. Of course, this is precisely how Paul is depicted in the legends. He travels from city to city dependent entirely on the hospitality of those who will receive him. When Onesiphorus, Paul's host in Iconium, follows him in leaving "the things of the world," the apostle must sell his coat to buy bread to keep from starving.

Such itinerant missionaries were active in Asia Minor throughout the first and second centuries. For example, the seer of the Apocalypse of John himself was a wandering prophet and belonged to a circle of prophets (Rev. 22:9). The seer also knew of Christian itinerants preaching rival messages (2:2). Furthermore, it would appear that these prophets, like Paul in our stories, maintained celibacy, for we are told that "those who follow the Lamb wherever he goes" are also those "who have not defiled themselves with women, for they are virgins" (14:4, marg.). Itinerant prophetism remained an important feature of the movement until the end of the second century when the episcopal arrangement replaced it.

Aristides was not the only person in the second century who identified the Cynic preacher with the Christian missionary. Even Christians sometimes confused the two, according to Lucian, a contemporary of Aristides and himself a rhetorician. He tells us that a Cynic named Peregrinus while visiting Palestine was mistaken for a Christian teacher. When Peregrinus was imprisoned for his association with the church, "people came even from *the cities of Asia,* sent by Christians at their common expense, to succour and defend and encourage the hero."[62]

One can easily see why itinerant preachers—whether Cynic or Christian—might understand themselves to be outside the social mainstream and detached from civic responsibilities. But even nonitinerant, resident Christians considered themselves "aliens" and "sojourners."[63] They were citizens of no earthly city or country. For example, Aviricius Marcellus, a Christian from Hieropolis, Phrygia, erected a tombstone which begins with the words: "I, a citizen of the elect city," thereby declaring himself to be a citizen of the heavenly Jerusalem.[64] One is reminded of the martyr Sanctus of Gaul, who answered every question about his name, race, city, and social standing with the same phrase "I am a Christian," *"Christianus sum."*[65] When the apologist Athenagoras and the *Epistle to*

Diognetus insist that it is the Christians who hold the empire together, they no doubt address those who saw the church endangering fundamental social institutions.[66]

Furthermore, Christians in Asia Minor seem to have understood their communities as political entities. The word *ekklēsia*, the most common designation for the Christian assembly, is an adopted political term for the voting assembly of the city, or *polis*. Christians also called themselves a "kingdom" (*basileia;* Rev. 1:5), a "chosen family, an imperial priesthood, a holy nationality" (1 Peter 2:9 influenced by Ex. 19:6, LXX), "fellow citizens" (Eph. 2:19), "the household of God" (1 Tim. 3:15), and "the family of the righteous" (*Martyrdom of Polycarp* 17:1). Christians referred to each other with familial titles such as "brother," "sister," and "children." Pagan resentment of these titles appropriated by the church was so strong that Tertullian felt obligated to address himself directly to the issue.[67]

But the controversy was not merely titular. The church as a social institution was indeed a new and disruptive element in Asia Minor. We must remember that apart from the synagogue the church as a closely knit, voluntary religious community had only remote analogies in the Greco-Roman world. Two prominent classicists have argued that the phenomenal success of the Christian movement in the second and third centuries was due in large part to the security provided by the strong social bonding available in the church as in almost no other contemporary institution.[68] The church provided services to its members which had been provided traditionally by the *polis* or the *oikia*. For example, the care of widows, usually the charge of the extended family, was now provided by the church.[69] There is little reason to doubt the claims of the apologist Aristides, who wrote early in the second century that Christians

> love one another, and from widows they do not turn away their esteem; and they deliver the orphan from him who treats him harshly. And he, who has, gives to him who has not, without boasting. And when they see a stranger, they take him in to their homes and rejoice over him as a very brother; for they do not call them brethren after the flesh, but brethren after the spirit and in God. And whenever one of their poor passes from the world, each one of them according to his ability gives heed to him and carefully sees to his burial.[70]

William M. Ramsay discovered in Phrygian funerary inscriptions evidence that Christians did indeed look after the burial of their own—

and in a manner that symbolizes how the church became an alternative to the household. Traditionally the residents of Phrygia buried their dead in family tombs and often posted warnings (some of which still exist) against tampering with the graves or burying others there. But among the Christian inscriptions, Ramsay found a substantial percentage that grant permission for the burial of nonfamily members.[71] Two of these inscriptions are particularly noteworthy. In the first a Christian man named Zosimus dedicates a tomb to himself, his wife, and his mother-in-law, who under most circumstances would have been buried in the tomb of her father, Skymnos, a wealthy pagan. Thus Ramsay suggests:

> The remarkable fact that Aurelia Flavia was buried in her son-in-law's tomb may . . . be explained as due to her religion. She and her daughter were Christians, but the family of Skymnos were pagans, and she preferred to be buried apart from her own family.[72]

Confirmation of this hypothesis comes from the second Christian inscription, which grants burial rights either to the women Ammia and Tatiana or to their husbands. Unfortunately, the inscription is ambiguous at this point. But no matter which is the proper interpretation, the inscription allows their spouses to be buried in the same tomb only if the spouses "hold to God." That is, burial in the tomb is contingent on a common faith and is not restricted to one household.[73]

The hostility caused by this shift of responsibility from the household to the church was exacerbated by the expectations of some churches that their members be celibate. We find this expectation over and over again in our legends: "There is no resurrection for you, except ye remain chaste and do not defile the flesh, but keep it pure" (*AP* 3:12). After his conversion even the baptized lion rejects the temptations of a frolicksome female feline. Of course, such requirements of continence promised to undermine the *oikia*, and as Jérôme Carcopino has shown, threats to the household in this period caused public outrage throughout the empire.[74] In fact, so important was the household that some Greek cities maintained ancient laws forbidding celibacy.[75] Such a law seems to be operative in the Thecla story when the governor asks her, "Why dost thou not marry Thamyris according to the law of the Iconians?"

There is also evidence to suggest that some Christians in Asia Minor challenged the institution of slavery which was so essential to the *oikia* and to the entire economic system. Paul himself had written a letter to Philemon of Colossae on behalf of Onesimus, Philemon's runaway slave. It is not clear whether Paul wanted him to free Onesimus or to commission him to accompany Paul and minister to him at Philemon's expense. Regardless, it is clear that Paul thinks Philemon must reevaluate the status of Onesimus now that he has become a Christian. If the Onesimus mentioned by Ignatius is the same person, Philemon apparently did free him, for Ignatius says he was the bishop of the church in Ephesus.[76] Clearly, slaves were permitted to be church officers, for the two leaders of the church in Bithynia whom Pliny tortured were female slaves.[77] According to Ignatius, some slaves acquired manumission through the generosity of fellow believers.[78] The Apocalypse of John castigates the empire for trafficking in slaves, "that is, human souls" (Rev. 18:13). Our legends also reveal a sensitivity to slaves in their concern for the poor, in their severe criticism of wealth, and in the prominence they give slaves, such as Eubula, Patroclus, and the maidservants of Theocleia and Tryphaena.

But according to the legends, the disruption of the household is not primarily related to the liberation of slaves but the liberation of women. For example, in the story about Thecla, when she becomes a Christian, "those who were in the house wept bitterly, Thamyris for the loss of a wife, Theocleia for that of a daughter, the maidservants for that of a mistress. So there was a great confusion of mourning in the house" (*AP* 3:10).[79]

Christian women who left the household often formed households of their own. For example, in Acts 9:36–42 Tabitha belongs to a circle of widows whom she supplied with clothes. The *Acts of Thomas* tells us that Thomas gathered the widows "together in the cities, and to them all he sent what was necessary by his deacons, both clothing and provisions for their nourishment."[80] The *Acts of Peter* mentions a Marcellus who supported widows in his home.[81] To be sure, we must be cautious in accepting any of the stories in these *Acts* as historically reliable, but they clearly are not fabricating the existence of such widow houses. Sozomen mentions the establishment of houses for widows and virgins by Eleusis of Cyzicus (fourth century) as though it were nothing out of the ordinary.[82] It is not clear from our three legends that celibate women formed such communities, but in another section of the *Acts of Paul* widows are treated as a distinct group within the church.[83]

The radical reordering of the lives of women who chose to live outside the *oikia* system is treated with great sensitivity in the depiction of Thecla's relationships with her mother, Theocleia, who demands Thecla's death, and to Tryphaena, who becomes like a mother to Thecla and tries to save her from death. Theocleia's violent response to Thecla's desertion is understandable when we keep in mind the economically precarious status of single women in most ancient societies. Except for the wealthy, single women were likely to become destitute unless they could establish some relationship with an *oikia,* usually with their relatives, and in the case of widows, frequently with their children. The number of times Greek and Jewish sources mention widows along with orphans as prime candidates for charity indicates that not all such women were successful in identifying with a household. Like orphans, they were anomalies to the basic socioeconomic arrangement.

Theocleia apparently was a widow, and if Thecla had married wealthy Thamyris, he would have supported his widowed mother-in-law. But when Thecla runs off after Paul, thereby declaring her independence from the *oikia* system, her mother loses both a child and a source of economic security. When Thecla returns to Iconium, she finds her mother and tries to convince her that her anxieties were misplaced: "Whether thou dost desire money, the Lord will give it thee through me; or thy child, see, I stand beside thee" (*AP* 3:43). In other words, by joining the Christian community Theocleia will receive the very forms of security available in the *oikia.* Once again, the church appears to have been an alternative household.

Thecla can offer her mother this security because she had been given charge of distributing to the poor the goods of Queen Tryphaena, also a widow, but so wealthy that she retained a staff of household slaves. Tryphaena adopts Thecla as her own daughter in place of her deceased natural daughter and provides Thecla with food, shelter, companionship, and whatever else she needs. Tryphaena functions as a model for other wealthy Christian women, encouraging them to use their means to support those women, who, having devoted themselves to celibacy, might be in danger of destitution. Surely this sensitivity to the economic vulnerability of women suggests that the legends reflect a woman's point of view.

Why did women turn their backs on their households in favor of the risks of poverty and the hostilities of their families? It is difficult to answer this question from second-century sources, but Rosemary Radford Ruether has answered it admirably from later ones. According to her analysis, asceticism was a

> liberating choice for women in the fourth century, for not only did it allow women to throw off the traditional female roles, but it offered female-directed communities where they could pursue the highest self-development as autonomous persons. It also offered security, for wealthy women endowed these communities for themselves and others. As a result, throngs of women were attracted to asceticism at this time.[84]

This interpretation of celibacy as independence differed radically from some male interpretations. Ruether shows that the great number of women in the fourth century who left their families in pursuit of the ascetic life created "a very real pastoral problem."

> Thus, for example, we find Augustine writing to a certain self-willed African matron, Ecducia, who had exacted a vow of continence from her husband and had begun to act with that liberty to dispose of her person and property autonomously befitting one whom the converted life had restored to equivalency with the male! . . . Since her husband had once consented, Augustine gives permission for her to continue in the life of continence, but reproves her severely for acting with independence in the disposal of her property and her personal conduct of life, which is incompatible with the nature of a woman, who does not have her own "head" but belongs to her husband, who is her "head."[85]

Some men of the period, however, recognized the importance of celibacy for freeing women from domestic restrictions, and applauded it. In an encomium to Thecla by an unknown author known to us as Pseudo-Chrysostom we find a passage amazingly sympathetic to the undesirable state of women in ancient households:

> [Thecla] had nothing in common with the earth, no connection with marital necessities, such as bearing up against a fornicating bridegroom, depriving oneself of the authority for making useful personal advancements, preparing food, when dressed up being the object of jealousy, being spat on before giving birth, as if she were not yet a married woman, and after having borne children, finding legal charges against herself on behalf of the children. And should a female be born? Her husband fumes because she was not male. And should a male also be born? [Her husband fumes] because the child was not good looking. And if both children should be graced with beauty? [Her husband fumes] because the pain of caring for them outweighs the benefits. Have they stopped nursing? Next comes the agony of rearing them. When they are healthy, there is fear lest they get sick. When they are sick, there is dread lest they die. When they die, there is fear that there will be disdain at one's ultimate childless state. When they do not die, there is the even weightier concern about those who live: whence the means for their children's education? Whence the preparations for their marriage contracts? Whence the beauty of their clothing? Whence the distribution of goods to each of the children? How much of one's goods

should be assigned to the older? How will one heal the hurts of the envious younger child?

In fact, virginity rendered Thecla untouched by the curses given to Eve.

> For the text that reads "your turning shall be to your husband, and he shall rule over you" is powerless with respect to those not lorded over by husbands. The passage "she shall bear children in sorrows" does not apply to those who live as virgins, for she who does not bear children is outside the sentence of terrible labor pains.[86]

Of course, one may argue that writings from the fourth and fifth centuries cannot be used to establish conditions in the second. However, the image of Thecla in the stories encourages just such aspirations to sexual equality and independence. She takes on male dress and assumes male responsibilities, such as teaching and disposing of Tryphaena's estate. Moreover, women in the fourth century who espoused celibacy were considered "new Theclas,"[87] and appropriately so. "Thecla was indeed an audacious role model for the Christian women. Her life clearly demonstrates that obedience to Christ can sanction sweeping disobedience to the established order of family and state."[88]

If our arguments in this chapter have been correct, it would appear that our stories were indeed "old wives' tales," told primarily by celibate women outside the *oikia*, hostile to Rome, and alienated from Asia Minor society. In the next chapter we shall see that the author of the Pastoral Epistles knew these stories, knew they were told by women, and knew that there was no more effective way of silencing them than writing in Paul's own name.

CHAPTER III

The Pastoral Epistles
Against "Old Wives' Tales"

Even though each of the Pastoral Epistles bears Paul's name, they are pseudonymous; their author is anonymous.[1] But if not by Paul, then where, when, and by whom were they written?

We have no external evidence of the letters before the last quarter of the second century;[2] therefore, they could have been written as late as the middle of that century but more probably sometime between 100 and 140. Whatever their date, they undoubtedly were written from Asia Minor, for the letters are saturated with personal and place names identified with the subcontinent. Two of the letters are addressed to Timothy, who, according to the Acts of the Apostles, was a native of Lystra, was known to the church in Iconium, and accompanied Paul through Phrygia, Galatia, and provincial Asia (Acts 16:1–11). According to 1 Tim. 1:3, Paul left Timothy in Ephesus to lead the church there. Furthermore, in 2 Tim. 1:15 we find a reference to Asia; in 1:18 to Ephesus; in 3:11 to Antioch, Iconium, and Lystra; in 4:10–13 to Galatia, Ephesus, and Troas; and in 4:20 to Miletus.

To be sure, the mere concentration of Asia Minor place-names is no guarantee of their Asian origin, but several other factors contribute to make this judgment almost certain. Hans von Campenhausen has demonstrated that the ecclesiastical organization, the theological postures, and the social issues addressed in the Pastoral Epistles were all present when Polycarp, bishop of Smyrna, wrote his letter to the Philippians.[3] In fact, so impressed was Von Campenhausen by these similarities that he claimed Polycarp wrote the Pastoral Epistles as well. Even though this thesis goes far beyond the evidence,[4] Von Campenhausen's sharp eye for similarities between Polycarp and the Pastoral Epistles has helped to establish their second-century Asia Minor setting.

Several other scholars have tried to peek behind the author's mask and have claimed the author was not Polycarp but was the same person who wrote Luke–Acts.[5] Ironically, some of the most telling arguments against this theory are the special conditions given by those who defend it in order to make it plausible.[6] But even if one granted these conditions—which I do not—one still could not account for other differences between Luke–Acts and the Pastoral Epistles, such as their contradictory assessments of celibacy (cf. Luke 20:34–35 and 1 Tim. 4:3). We shall probably never know the identity of the author. He must remain masked and unnamed. But the very fact that he chose to mask himself as Paul reveals much about what he hoped his letters would accomplish.

Pseudonymity, or writing in another's name, was a widespread early Christian practice, especially in the Pauline tradition. In addition to the Pastoral Epistles we know of correspondence between Paul and Seneca, an *Epistle to the Laodiceans,* a third letter to the Corinthians, a *Prayer of the Apostle Paul,* and an *Apocalypse of Paul.* The New Testament books Ephesians, Colossians, and 2 Thessalonians also probably are pseudonymous. But while there is little doubt that pseudonymity was a popular early Christian literary exercise, there remains a vigorous debate over its legitimacy. To some it simply was a means by which unoriginal minds attempted to give authority to writings otherwise devoid of it, and as such, pseudonymity was a deceptive and deleterious development in the history of the church.[7] Even in antiquity some rejected pseudonymity as a despicable deception, though there were still times when they recognized it as legitimate.[8] In the Hellenistic world, pseudonymity was a school exercise whereby a student attempted to demonstrate a mastery of the style, vocabulary, and philosophical perspectives of a venerated author.[9]

Other scholars have argued that pseudonymity not only was a legitimate literary activity but was consistent with the very nature of early Christian experience. According to some, authors who wrote under a pseudonym did so as the result of ecstatic inspiration in which they became identified with the spirit of another.[10] Others suggest that pseudonymity was the "logical conclusion of the presupposition that the Spirit himself [sic!] was the real author." Out of deference to "the authentic witness, the Holy Spirit, the Lord, and the apostles" the author chose not to write in his own name.[11] According to others, pseudonymity reflects an author's belief that he had been sent out on his mission in the name of an apostle and therefore was justified in writing in that name.[12] Recently several German scholars have championed yet another explanation of pseudonymity: the author recognized the normative value of a certain period in the past for the self-understanding of his community, and by writing in the name of someone from that period he attempted to "personalize the tradition." Pseudonymity, therefore, represents a kind of "transsubjectivity" in that it reclaims the foundational period by identifying with one important figure of that time, and by translating the perspective of that figure into the new situation of the church.[13]

Each of these positive evaluations of pseudonymity downplays the relevance of intra-Christian disputes over the legacy of the apostles which characterized the church of the first two centuries. Paul was a hero not only in that tradition of the church which ultimately became dominant but also among Christian Gnostics, Marcionites, and Montanists. The author of 2 Peter, writing around 150, complains about opponents who twist Paul's letter to support their own positions and who apparently were successful in carrying away many people from the author's religious community (2 Peter 3:15–17).

Consequently, some interpreters have preferred to explain the Pauline facade of the Pastoral Epistles as a literary device for convincing readers that the author's understanding of Paul was the correct one. This explanation accounts for the insistence throughout the letters that they were indeed from Paul's own hand. More than any other pseudo-Pauline document—canonical or noncanonical—the letters struggle to pass themselves off as authentic. Over and over again the author alludes to places, people, and events traditionally identified with the apostle; for example, we find twenty-seven different names of Paul's associates compressed into these three short letters. But if we are to be more precise about the function of this Pauline disguise, we must identify the false teachers against whom the letters were written.

Fully one fifth of the Pastoral Epistles directly refutes false teachers, and many other passages do so indirectly.[14] From this quantity of material one might assume that identifying these opponents would be easy, but the contrary is true. Few issues in the interpretation of these letters have proved as baffling or controversial as describing these elusive foes. The confusion is due to two factors: first, only once does the author engage his opponents in direct theological discourse (1 Tim. 4:1–5); otherwise he resorts to name-calling.[15] Second, it is difficult to identify all the refutations with the characteristics of a single opponent. Those who do so frequently create some unnatural hybrid, like Werner Georg Kümmel's limping centaur: "Jewish-Christian, Gnostic."[16] John J. Gunther lists nineteen different scholarly hypotheses for the identification of these opponents.[17]

Probably it is more nearly correct to think that the Pastoral Epistles oppose false teachers of various kinds: Gnostics (1 Tim. 6:20; cf. 1:3–11; 2 Tim. 2:14–19), Jewish Christians (Titus 1:10–16), and perhaps Marcionites.[18] But there is yet another opponent denounced in the letters who seldom has been identified: Paul himself as depicted in the legend tradition.

THE FALSE TEACHERS AND THE LEGENDARY PAUL

Many characteristics of the false teachers are identical with those of Paul in the legends. For example, in 2 Tim. 3:6–7 Paul commands Timothy to avoid those

> who make their way into households and capture weak women, burdened with sins and swayed by various impulses, who will listen to anybody and can never arrive at a knowledge of the truth.

The word rendered by the Revised Standard Version as "capture" more literally means "to take prisoner of war." The imagery therefore is of missionaries who, like soldiers, enter households and carry off "little women" *(gynaikaria)* as prisoners. This is precisely what Paul does with Thecla, Artemilla, and Eubula in the *Acts of Paul,* all of whom leave their lovers to follow the apostle. But in the Pastoral Epistles such women must not leave their households to follow teachers, for they will never comprehend the truth. Instead of responding rationally, they are driven about by base impulses and are burdened down with unnecessary guilt—presumably guilt related to sexual activity and desires.

This concern for the welfare of the household also appears in Titus 1:10–15, where the opponents are accused of "upsetting whole households by teaching for base gain what they have no right to teach" (v. 11). In v. 15 we see that one aspect of their teaching was asceticism: "To the pure all things are pure, but to the corrupt and unbelieving nothing is pure; their very minds and consciences are corrupted."

In 1 Timothy 4 we find another passage objecting to the asceticism of the false teachers:

> Now the Spirit expressly says that in later times some will depart from the faith by giving heed to deceitful spirits and doctrines of demons, through the pretentions of liars whose consciences are seared, who forbid marriage and enjoin abstinence from foods which God created to be received with thanksgiving by those who believe and know the truth. (1 Tim. 4:1–3)

Obviously the author would have had little sympathy with the Paul of the *Acts of Paul* for whom chastity was a requirement for resurrection (*AP* 3:12; cf. 3:5). But this passage also contradicts the Paul of the *Acts of Paul* at two other points.

First, in the *Acts of Paul* the apostle is a vegetarian and a teetotaler. Even the Eucharist consists of bread and water instead of wine. The author of the Pastorals, on the other hand, opposes such abstinence from foods and in fact tells Timothy, "No longer drink only water, but use a little wine for the sake of your stomach" (1 Tim. 5:23).

Second, the author claims that the opponents' teaching of asceticism was inspired by "deceitful spirits and doctrines of demons," and not by the Holy Spirit, whom he enlists for his own position: "The Spirit expressly says. . . ." Presumably, the opponents legitimated their asceticism by claims of inspiration, or their inspiration by their asceticism. Both are closely related in the *Acts of Paul* and in the communities in which they most likely were told. In the Thecla story we are told that it is to the continent that God will speak (*AP* 3:5). Thus, throughout the legends those who see visions or speak in the Spirit are the continent, like Paul, Thecla, and the prophetess Myrta.

This association of celibacy with revelation characterizes Montanism. According to the prophetess Priscilla: "[Sexual] purity is harmonious, and they see visions; and, turning their face downward, they even hear manifest voices."[19] Presumably, this is why Montanus annulled marriages at the outbreak of the New Prophecy in central Asia Minor early in the second half of the second century. Both Maximilla and Priscilla deserted their husbands after they received their prophetic gifts, and the Montanist prophet Proclus maintained his virginity until his death. Epiphanius says that Quintillian assemblies commenced with a procession of prophesying virgins.[20]

The author of the Pastorals tries to break this bond between prophecy and celibacy in three ways. First, as we have seen, the Spirit condemns such celibacy as demonic. Second, celibacy and dietary restrictions, instead of attesting a strong and sensitive conscience, attest a conscience either cauterized and thus insensitive to right and wrong, or branded and thus owned by demonic powers. Third, the author accuses the opponents of lying, which may mean nothing more than that they claimed divine approval for their asceticism when in fact they had none. But it could also mean that these opponents told legends about Paul which depicted him as an ascetic. Notice that this passage against celibate prophets continues through vs. 7 and 8, where the author warns Timothy to avoid "old wives' tales."

> Avoid the profane tales told by old women. Rather train yourself toward godliness. For training of the body profits little, but piety is profitable in every way.

If, as many interpreters have suggested,[21] the bodily training opposed here refers to ascetic disciplines, it would confirm our thesis that the liars in v. 2 who forbid marriage should be identified with the women in v. 7 who told stories. To the women these stories were sacred legends; to the author of the Pastorals they were sinister lies.

Nowhere is the disagreement between our legends and the Pastorals more apparent than in 1 Tim. 2:11–15:

> Let a woman learn in silence with all submissiveness. I permit no woman to teach or to have authority over men; she is to keep silent. For Adam was formed first, then Eve; and Adam was not deceived, but the woman was deceived and became a transgressor. Yet woman will be saved through bearing children, if they continue in faith and love and holiness, with modesty.

In the legends, Paul commissions a woman to teach, here he forbids it. In the legends, Paul tells women that only the continent will be saved, here he tells women they shall be saved by bearing children. Instead of luring Thecla away from her lover and encouraging her to teach the word of God, the author of the Pastorals indicates that Paul would have had her marry, be submissive to her husband, raise lots of children, and live happily—in silent domestication—ever after.

In addition to these obvious disagreements between the legends and the Pastoral Epistles there also are many similarities which make it likely that the author knew our legends at some stage in their oral transmission.

THE *ACTS OF PAUL* AND THE PASTORAL EPISTLES

Certain references to Paul's associates and experiences in the Pastoral Epistles cannot be accounted for in terms of independent historical reminiscences of events in Paul's life, nor in terms of dependence on the Acts of the Apostles or on Paul's own letters. Therefore, unless the author fabricated these names and episodes, he probably learned of them through oral channels. I shall attempt to show that because many of these names and episodes appear in the *Acts of Paul* as well as in the Pastoral Epistles, and because literary dependence of one of these documents on the other must be ruled highly unlikely, it would appear that both authors knew the same oral legends about Paul.

In the Thecla story Paul travels with Demas and Hermogenes to Iconium, where they are entertained by Onesiphorus and his family. Later, Demas and Hermogenes desert Paul for a bribe, but the household of Onesiphorus remains faithful to Paul, even though he is imprisoned. Compare these events with 2 Tim. 1:15–18, where the two devious fellow missionaries are not Demas and Hermogenes but Phygelus and Hermogenes:

> You are aware that all who are in *Asia* turned away from me, and among them Phygelus and *Hermogenes.* May the Lord grant mercy to the household of *Onesiphorus,* for he often refreshed me; he was not ashamed of my chains, but when he arrived in Rome he searched for me eagerly and found me— may the Lord grant him to find mercy from the Lord on that Day—and you well know all the service he rendered at Ephesus. (Italics added)

Only in the *Acts of Paul* and the Pastorals in all of early Christian literature do we find a reference to Onesiphorus, and in both he is identified with Asia Minor, in both he befriends Paul during a time of imprisonment, and in both he always appears with his family. Likewise, only in the *Acts* and in the Pastorals do we find a reference to Hermogenes, and in both he is twinned with a companion and deserts Paul in Asia Minor. Even though in the Pastorals Hermogenes is not accompanied by Demas, the author also knows of Demas' desertion: "Demas, in love with this present world, has deserted me" (2 Tim. 4:10a). Philemon, v. 24 and Colossians 4:14 also mention Demas, but only in the *Acts of Paul* and the Pastorals does he desert Paul, and in both his motivation for doing so is greed. In the *Acts of Paul,* Demas and Hermogenes tell Thamyris that the resurrection already has taken place. The only other place in all of early Christian literature where two persons make this claim is in the Pastorals, where Hymenaeus and Philetus are said to have "swerved from the truth by holding that the resurrection is past already. They are upsetting the faith of some" (2 Tim. 2:17–18).

In the *Acts of Paul,* Paul and Thecla leave Iconium, travel toward Lystra, and arrive in Antioch, where Alexander opposes Paul and tries to kill Thecla. The only other reference to an Alexander opposing Paul is in the Pastorals:[22]

> Alexander the coppersmith did me great harm; the Lord will requite him for his deeds. Beware of him yourself, for he strongly opposed our message. (2 Tim. 4:14–15; cf. 1 Tim. 1:19–20)

It would appear that here, as in the *Acts of Paul,* Alexander is a threat to the Pauline mission in Asia Minor, for Timothy is warned to watch out for him in Ephesus.

Further evidence that the author knew of these events in Iconium, Lystra, and Antioch comes from 2 Tim. 3:10–11:

> Now you have observed my teaching, my conduct, my aim in life, my faith, my patience, my love, my steadfastness, my persecutions, my sufferings, what befell me at Antioch, at Iconium, and at Lystra, what persecutions I endured; yet from them all the Lord rescued me.

The Acts of the Apostles also mentions Paul's persecutions in these three cities; therefore, one might argue, the parallels between the *Acts of Paul* and the Pastorals could be explained in terms of a shared knowledge of the canonical Acts. However, the Acts and the *Acts of Paul* share nothing in common regarding the circumstances of Paul's persecutions. Likewise, in the Pastorals, Paul reminds Timothy that he "has observed" these persecutions, but in Acts they all take place prior to Paul meeting Timothy (Acts 16:1–3). If the authors of the *Acts of Paul* and of the Pastorals knew the canonical Acts, they certainly did not take efforts to make their accounts conform with it. Probably we should explain these parallels between the *Acts of Paul* and the Pastorals as we would the others which obviously cannot be attributed to a shared knowledge of Acts.

In Chapter I, we saw the similarities between the story of the baptized lion and the Pastorals.[23] According to the *Acts of Paul*, while Paul was staying with Priscilla and Aquila in Ephesus, "all the house of Ammia turned against Paul, that he might die." Without any comrade to lend support, Paul gives a bold witness before the governor and a crowd of spectators. The governor condemns him to be eaten by a ferocious lion, but the lion miraculously refuses to eat him, and both flee the scene unharmed. Compare this with 2 Tim. 4:16–19:

> At my first defense no one took my part; all deserted me. May it not be charged against them! But the Lord stood by me and gave me strength to proclaim the message fully, that all the Gentiles might hear it. So I was rescued from the lion's mouth. The Lord will rescue me from every evil and save me for his heavenly kingdom. To him be the glory for ever and ever. Amen. Greet Prisca and Aquila, and the household of Onesiphorus.

Three features are common to both accounts: Paul's friends in Ephesus include Priscilla and Aquila; Paul gives his defense alone before a crowd of Gentiles; and he is saved from a lion.

It is more difficult to find evidence of some genetic connection between the Pastoral Epistles and the martyrdom story, but there does appear to be one point of contact. 2 Timothy 4:10–11a reads: "For Demas, in love with this present world, has deserted me and gone to Thessalonica; Crescens has gone to Galatia [several texts read "Gaul"], Titus to Dalmatia. Luke alone is with me." Compare this with the *Acts of Paul,* where we are told that when Paul arrived in Rome: "There were awaiting Paul at Rome Luke from Gaul and Titus from Dalmatia" (11:1). In both the *Acts of Paul* and the Pastoral Epistles, Luke and Titus accompany Paul in Rome; in both, Titus is associated with Dalmatia; and, if one prefers the reading "Gaul" in 2 Tim. 4:10, in both, one of Paul's companions is a missionary to Gaul. In no other early Christian document do we find a mission of Paul's associates to either Dalmatia or Gaul. Nowhere else is Titus related to Dalmatia or present with Paul in Rome.[24]

Surely this large number of parallels between the *Acts of Paul* and the Pastoral Epistles is not coincidental. The first scholars to recognize these similarities assumed they were best explained as independent reminiscences of historical events. In the fifth century an unknown Christian author (later called Ambrosiaster) wrote a commentary on 2 Timothy in which he notes that the characters Alexander, Demas, and Hermogenes are mentioned in "other scriptures,"[25] no doubt referring to the *Acts of Paul.* Five or six centuries later another unknown scholar added to his copy of 2 Timothy, after "what befell me in Antioch," in 3:11 the words "those things he suffered on Thecla's behalf." Again in 4:19 he added the names of Onesiphorus' family members ("Lectra his wife and Simmias and Zeno his children"), which must have come from the *Acts of Paul.*[26]

Modern scholars, however, agree that the similarities between the *Acts of Paul* and the Pastoral Epistles cannot be explained as independent testimonies to historical events, but they do not agree as to which of three basic models best explains the relationship: (1) the author of the *Acts of Paul* knew and used the Pastorals; (2) the author of the Pastorals knew and used a written source behind the *Acts of Paul;* or (3) both authors knew and used the same oral traditions.

MODEL ONE: THE AUTHOR OF THE *ACTS OF PAUL*
KNEW AND USED THE PASTORALS

This has been the overwhelmingly favorite model of the persons who have addressed themselves to the question. Into this category fall most of those who attribute the Pastorals to Paul himself or who date them to the first century, but this also has been the model chosen by some of the finest critical students of Christian antiquities.[27] At first glance this judgment would seem quite justified inasmuch as the *Acts of Paul* almost certainly was written after the Pastorals. But a closer investigation reveals that even though this model can account for the similarities between the documents, it makes little sense of the differences.

Richard Adelbert Lipsius preferred model one and attempted to account for these differences as follows:

> A Gnostic writer of that time contrasted a Paul conforming to the bias of his Gnostic associates over against a Paul of the Pastoral Letters. Thus the anti-Gnostic image of Paul in the Pastoral Letters is toned down by the representation in these Acts, which is so thoroughly grounded in Gnostic assumptions.[28]

But Lipsius is incorrect on two counts. First, it must be judged highly unlikely that the *Acts of Paul* ever was Gnostic. The glorification of martyrdom, the concern for the body in preparation for the resurrection, the apocalyptic destruction of the world, and the attribution of the creation to God all tell against a Gnostic hypothesis. Second, the claim that the *Acts of Paul* contains a polemic against a rival image of Paul is unlikely. Peter Corssen opposed Lipsius at this point:

> Lipsius' judgment concerning the relationship of the Acts to the Timothy correspondence is entirely wrong, inferring that a Gnostic writer wanted to contrast "a Paul conforming to the bias of his Gnostic associates over against a Paul of the Pastoral letters." The relationship is just the converse. To the extent that the Timothy correspondence is tendentious, such tendentiousness is correspondingly lacking in the Acts and the tendentiousness of the former is in large part directed against views in which the later is rooted.[29]

Surely Corssen is right in identifying the direction of the polemic in this manner, as the very genres of the *Acts of Paul* and the Pastorals indicate. If someone wanted to alter the traditional memory of a historical figure, he or she would be more likely to use forged letters than a collection of stories: discourse in the first person ("I") carries authority impossible in the third ("he"). Furthermore, if the author of the *Acts of Paul* had wanted to refute the picture of Paul in the Pastorals, we would expect to find him authenticating the narrative in order to secure credulity over against the epistolary opposition. He might have written in the first person plural ("we"), thereby implying he himself had been present. Or he might have said, "Paul himself told this to X, who told it to me," or the like. We find none of this. On the other hand, the

Pastorals are adamantly, consistently, and even tediously pseudony-mous. If the polarized depictions of Paul in the Pastorals and in the *Acts of Paul* reflect a battle for Paul's memory, it is likely that the pseudony-mous epistle, being the sharper weapon, would have been chosen by the aggressor. If such an epistle were judged authentic, no story could supersede its depiction. Model one invariably wrecks upon this shoal, because it misjudges the direction of the polemical currents.

MODEL TWO: THE AUTHOR OF THE PASTORALS
USED A WRITTEN SOURCE BEHIND THE *ACTS OF PAUL*

Many scholars, including both Lipsius and Corssen, have argued that behind the *Acts of Paul* lay an earlier written version of the story of Thecla.[30] In fact, one scholar goes so far as to suggest that this hypothetical text is "the earliest Christian document we possess."[31] Corssen seems to have thought that if indeed there were such a document, the author of the Pastorals may well have known it and consequently may have written in Paul's name to oppose it. Unfortunate-ly, he never developed this hypothesis systematically. The only scholar who did so was Hans Helmut Mayer.[32]

Mayer agreed with Corssen that the Pastoral Epistles were directed against the depiction of Paul in an earlier version of the Thecla story, but he was not convinced that Corssen's orientation could account for the similarities between the documents. Would someone interested in op-posing a document incorporate into his own work so many of the same *dramatis personae?* Mayer answered: No! Rather, the version of the Pastorals we now have has been doctored up by a later hand. The original version did not contain the names Onesiphorus, Demas, Her-mogenes, and Alexander. Later these names were inserted into the text for purposes of illustration by someone who knew the Thecla story and was unaware of the polemic against the story in the original version of the Pastorals.[33]

Though ingenious, this explanation almost certainly is wrong. One need not speculate about hypothetical earlier versions of the *Acts of Paul* and the Pastorals in order to describe the relationship between them. By so doing, Mayer provided Johannes Rohde with an irresistible and vulnerable target, and allowed him cogently to reaffirm the first mod-el.[34] No one has reopened the case since Rohde published his rebuttal in 1968.

But the case must be reopened. Model one and model two both share a serious and devastating flaw: each insists on explaining the relation-ship between the documents solely in terms of written dependence.

Neither considers the possible role of oral tradition. Even though no previous scholar has recommended the third of our models, it is the one that best accounts for the evidence.

MODEL THREE: THE AUTHORS KNEW THE SAME ORAL LEGENDS

Since, as we have seen, the *Acts of Paul* is heavily dependent on oral legends known in Asia Minor early in the second century, it certainly is possible that they also were known to the author of the Pastoral Epistles, and if so, he certainly would have objected to their depiction of Paul. Apparently he saw in them what one folklorist has called "the doctrinally polluting substance of oral traditions,"[35] and wrote in Paul's name to correct them.

Obviously, this hypothesis can account for the different depictions of Paul in the *Acts of Paul* and the Pastorals without conjecturing earlier written sources, but it also can better account for the similarities than either of the other models. Those who attempt to explain the parallels in terms of literary dependence must somehow explain why they are not exact. For example, in the *Acts of Paul*, Hermogenes is associated with Demas; in the Pastorals, with Phygelus. In the *Acts of Paul*, Onesiphorus' home is in Iconium; in the Pastorals, in Ephesus. Rohde tries to solve this problem simply by claiming that the author of the *Acts of Paul* was arbitrary and imprecise in his use of the Pastorals.[36] But if one explains the relationship in terms of a common knowledge of oral tradition, these variations can be attributed to the vagaries of the storytelling process. Substitutions of personal and place names are characteristic of oral transmission, inasmuch as names are epiphenomena to the story: they can be interchanged without fundamentally altering its texture or meaning.

Furthermore, if we assume that this third model is the most adequate, we are able to see how the author of the Pastorals brilliantly exploited the epistolary genre. That is, it would appear that in order to combat the image of Paul in the legend tradition he incorporated into his epistles three rhetorical features heretofore foreign to the genre. First, the author wrote 2 Timothy as though it were Paul's last testament. Shortly before his death Paul reflects on his life, foresees the state of the church in the future, and interprets the circumstances of his death. Second, the author has Paul write to two individuals and by so doing can develop these characters as well as Paul; hence, some scholars speak of "double pseudonymity" in the Pastorals.[37] Third, he incorporates into 1 Timothy and Titus lists of qualifications for bishops, presbyters, deacons, and widows by means of which he presents his idealizations of church leaders in his own day. The author uses each of these three rhetorical devices in order to bend Pauline tradition toward social conservatism.

BOGUS LETTERS AND SOCIAL COMPLIANCE

PAUL: THE SUBMISSIVE MARTYR

In 2 Timothy the epistle provides the literary occasion for the author's version of Paul's final testament.[38] The apostle is in a Roman jail (2 Tim. 1:17), knows his death is near (4:6–8), and therefore writes his "son" Timothy his final instructions. Paul is accompanied only by Luke (4:11).[39] Demas had deserted Paul, and Crescens, Titus, Tychicus, Erastus, and Trophimus are on missions elsewhere (4:10, 12, 20). Onesiphorus had come to Rome, sought Paul out, and ministered to him (1:16–17), but now was back home in Ephesus (4:19). Paul therefore asks that Timothy come quickly and bring with him Mark, books, parchments, and a misplaced cloak, apparently to make his last days more stimulating and comfortable (4:11, 13).

Why this preoccupation with Paul's situation in Rome? It appears that the author wanted to draw an alternative image of the dying Paul to that drawn by the martyrdom story in the *Acts of Paul,* which bristles with anti-Roman hostility. That story depicts Nero as the archetypal Antichrist, and the empire as the diabolical counterpart to the kingdom of God. No one serves two masters in the story; they cannot serve both Christ and Caesar.

In 2 Timothy, on the other hand, we hear not so much as a whisper of criticism for Rome. Of course, the author considers Paul's execution a wicked act, but he adroitly prevents Paul's execution from becoming an anti-Roman symbol which could be used to stimulate political hostilities. We find no reference to Nero, to soldiers, or to the legal charges or proceedings against Paul. It almost appears that Rome was merely a passive instrument of God's will. God had rescued Paul in the past and could do so easily now if that were God's desire (3:10–11; 4:17–18). But sensing that his end is providentially near, he accepts it with stoic resignation:

> For I am already on the point of being sacrificed; the time of my departure has come. I have fought the good fight, I have finished the race, I have kept the faith. (4:6–7)

Even though Paul is "wearing fetters like a criminal," his imprisonment is not the result of antisocial conduct or of political opposition but of his preaching the gospel (1:8; 11–12; 2:9). Such sufferings are inevitable for anyone wishing to live a godly life (3:12). Nowhere do we find evidence that Paul had caused the Romans difficulty or that they were culpable for his death.

Confirmation of our claim concerning the ameliorating political sentiments behind 2 Timothy comes from passages in the other two Pastoral Epistles. In Titus 3:1–2, Paul commands Titus:

> Remind them to be submissive to rulers and authorities, to be obedient, to be ready for any honest work, to speak evil of no one, to avoid quarreling, to be gentle, and to show perfect courtesy toward all people.

Even more telling is 1 Tim. 2:1–2:

> First of all, then, I urge that supplications, prayers, intercessions, and thanksgivings be made for all people, on behalf of kings [i.e., emperors] and all who are in positions of authority so that we may lead a quiet and peaceful life in all piety and dignity.

The words "first of all" can indicate either that the injunction is of prime importance or that it is the first in a list of commands for the church which continue to 3:13. Even if one prefers the second meaning, the very fact that the author places the command to pray for authorities at the beginning of the list underlines its importance.

The author sees a relationship between these prayers and the tranquillity of the church, but it is not clear what that relationship is. Some have suggested that, as in a prayer for pagan authorities in 1 Clement 61, believers are to pray that the authorities may govern wisely and as a result of this wise governance the church would naturally be at peace.[40] Notice, however, that our passage includes, among other forms of prayer, thanksgiving for the authorities. This expression of appreciation for Rome suggests that the peace of the church depends not on the prayer for wise administration as much as on the act of prayer itself as a demonstration of goodwill toward the empire. This seems to be the idea behind Polycarp's command that Christians "pray also for kings and potentates and rulers and for those who persecute and hate you . . . that your fruit may be manifest to all" (Polycarp, *Philippians* 12:3). Likewise in 1 Peter we are told that by honoring and being subject to the emperor believers will put "to silence the ignorance of foolish" people (1 Peter 2:15). Tertullian and Justin Martyr, both with links to Asia Minor, cite prayers for the emperors as proofs of political cooperation.[41] So too in 1 Timothy: by praying and giving thanks for emperors, rulers, and all humankind Christians demonstrate to outsiders their respect for society at large. This cooperation with political power is epitomized in 2

Timothy by the depiction of Paul as a submissive martyr, resigned to his fate, and reconciled with Rome.

TIMOTHY AND TITUS: THE GUARDIANS OF THE TRADITION

Timothy and Titus are necessary links for establishing the continuity between Paul's authority and the authority of bishops in the author's own day. Six times in the Pastoral Epistles, Paul defends his apostleship by claiming that he was appointed to the office by God or Christ (1 Tim. 1:1, 12–16; 2:7; 2 Tim. 1:1, 11–12; Titus 1:1–3). The author did not include these repetitious defenses of Paul's apostleship in order to convince those doubting it. Rather, by establishing the divine origin of Paul's apostleship, and by having Paul transmit that authority to Timothy, Titus, and through them to later presbyter-bishops the author demonstrates the genealogical divine origin of the offices. As Werner Stenger has expressed it:

> The author projects the . . . function of the church official of his time in the images of Timothy and Titus—who function as "representatives" of the apostle already in the authentic Paulines—in order to make the apostle present when he himself cannot come. Thereby the author succeeded in building a literary bridge over the gap in time between Paul and the post-Pauline church, and to assert the presence of the apostle himself in the activity of church officers.[42]

Perhaps this is why Paul is the only apostle mentioned in the letters; it is through Paul alone that the authority of the presbyter-bishop is derived.

Timothy and Titus of all of Paul's associates mentioned in his undisputed letters are the best suited for expressing the author's idealization of the authentic Pauline lineage,[43] but in the Pastoral Epistles these two characters are further developed so as to epitomize the perfect church leader.

Timothy is presented as a weak, shy, and fearful youth whom the apostle must encourage to use his rightful authority and to be brave in the shadow of persecution (1 Tim. 4:12; 5:23; 2 Tim. 1:8; 2:1–7). But even though he is young, he is no neophyte. His mother and grandmother were both believers and taught him about the faith as a lad (2 Tim. 1:5; 3:15). Paul was present at Timothy's ordination when his divine selection was revealed to all: prophetic utterances pointed to him, God gave him a special gift, he gave a true confession, and the presbyters laid their hands on him (1 Tim. 1:18–20; 4:14; 6:12; 2 Tim. 1:5–7). Both Timothy and Titus were fellow missionaries with Paul until the apostle decided that for the benefit of local churches Timothy should stay in Ephesus and Titus in Crete, where they would ensure the dominance of true teaching and appoint other clergy (1 Tim. 1:3–4; Titus 1:5). In other words, Timothy and Titus are apostles who have become presbyter-bishops, itinerants who have become resident clergy, missionaries once dependent on Paul who are now independent.

Paul tells Titus that because he now has full independent authority he must be neither disregarded nor drawn into theological disputes (Titus 2:15; cf. 1:10–11). If someone disagrees with him and continues to be uncompliant after two rebukes, Titus must "have nothing more to do with him, knowing that such a person is perverted and sinful" (3:10–11). Likewise Timothy is told not to become embroiled in arguments but simply to pronounce the truth as he received it: "Have nothing to do with stupid, senseless controversies; you know that they breed quarrels" (2 Tim. 2:23). The author of the Pastorals apparently thought this imperious authority was necessary for ensuring the transmission of "sound doctrine" and the rejection of the insubordinate "who reject the truth" (Titus 1:9 to 2:1). Timothy is all the more capable of "guarding the truth" (2 Tim. 1:14) because he is educated, especially in the Scriptures (2 Tim. 3:15–17; cf. 1 Tim. 1:7; 4:13).

Timothy and Titus also have obligations outside the church in that they must be paradigms of social respectability. As Paul tells Titus:

> Show yourself in all respects a model of good deeds, and in your teaching show integrity, gravity, and sound speech that cannot be censured, so that an opponent may be put to shame, having nothing evil to say of us. (Titus 2:7–8)

How do these characterizations of Timothy and Titus relate to our thesis that the Pastorals were written to counteract the legend tradition? In the legends we find no mention whatever of bishops, presbyters, deacons, or other officers. This silence is striking when we recall that the author of the *Acts of Paul* was himself a presbyter and subject to the authority of a bishop. Furthermore, in the Philippi section of the *Acts of Paul* is a letter from the Corinthians to Paul written by a bishop Stephanus and four presbyters, and delivered to Paul by two deacons (*Acts of Paul* 8:1.1 and 2.1). In the legends, however, ecclesiastical authority is charismatic, itinerant, and relatively democratic, in contrast to the genetic, resident, and hierarchical authority of the Pastoral Epistles.

The letters of Ignatius allow us to see that the two rival models for ecclesiastical leadership were related to actual conditions in Asia Minor churches. Ignatius stayed for a period in Smyrna on his way to Rome for execution, and during this stay he was visited by bishops from Ephesus,

Magnesia, and Tralles (*Ephesians* 21:1; *Magnesians* 2:1; *Trallians* 1:1). Later while in Troas he was visited by the bishop of Philadelphia (*Philadelphians* 1:1). Ignatius sent each of these bishops home with a letter which in every case attempted to secure the position of the bishop in the church and to scold the insubordinate. To the Ephesians he wrote that they "should live in harmony with the will of the bishop" (*Ephesians* 4:1). To the Trallians he wrote: "Let all respect the deacons as Jesus Christ, even as the bishop is also a type of the Father, and the presbyters as the council of God and the college of apostles. Without these the name 'Church' is not given" (*Trallians* 3:1). To the Philadelphians he wrote: "For as many as belong to God and Jesus Christ,—these are with the bishop" (*Philadelphians* 3:2). Ignatius' instructions to the Magnesians are especially interesting because their bishop, Damas, was very young—like the Timothy of the Pastorals—and some seem to have presumed on his youth (*Magnesians* 3:1). Even though he is young, Ignatius says, all in the church must be in harmony "with the bishop presiding in the place of God, and the presbyters in the place of the council of the Apostles, and the deacons . . . entrusted with the service of Jesus Christ" (*Magnesians* 6:1). Likewise, to the Smyrneans Ignatius writes: "Let no one do any of the things appertaining to the church without the bishop" (*Smyrneans* 8:1). And when he writes to Polycarp, the bishop of Smyrna, Ignatius commands him to be a strong leader: "Stand firm as an anvil which is smitten" (*Polycarp* 3:1; cf. 2:3; 4:1). Apparently Polycarp was in fact an adamantine leader, for Ignatius' letter to him begins with a reference to his "godly mind which is fixed as if on an immoveable rock" (1:1). This repeated emphasis on the adamance and authority of the bishop in letters often brought to the churches by the bishops themselves suggests that not everyone was in fact obedient to them.

Perhaps now we can understand the importance of the characterizations of Timothy and Titus for counteracting the legend tradition. First, Timothy and Titus, as itinerants who became resident clergy, symbolize the full authority of resident leaders. It is the author's way of saying what the *Didache* says directly: "Do not despise them [i.e., bishops and deacons], for they are your honourable men together with the prophets and teachers" (*Didache* 15:2). Second, the author gives divine sanction to the church officials and thereby limits charismatic authority. Surely this is why he emphasized the role of the Holy Spirit in the ordination of Timothy, who was selected by prophetic utterance and was given a spiritual gift (1 Tim. 1:18; 4:14; 2 Tim. 1:6). Third, by giving authority to a local leader to settle disputes the author hopes both to guarantee the transmission of "sound doctrine" and to minimize theological controversies which to outsiders might appear senseless, trivial, and unnecessarily disruptive. Fourth, Timothy and Titus are models of social respectability. In them the author expresses the ideal to be desired of all other leaders. Needless to say, social respectability is not characteristic of Christian leaders in the legend tradition.

BISHOPS, PRESBYTERS, AND DEACONS: THE RESPECTABLE HOUSEHOLDERS

In addition to presenting Timothy and Titus as the original and ideal resident clergy, the author guarantees the good character of ecclesiastical leaders by altering the epistolary genre to include lists of qualifications for bishops (1 Tim. 3:1–7 and Titus 1:7–9), one short list for presbyters (Titus 1:5–6 and perhaps 2:2), one list for deacons (1 Tim. 3:8–13), and the longest list, including detailed instructions, pertains to the widows (1 Tim. 5:3–16). Because the office of widows presented the author with a particular problem, we shall analyze this passage in detail later. In the present context we shall refer to the widows only when their qualifications are germane to those for other offices.

Most of the qualifications are interchangeable from office to office; therefore, it would appear that instead of lists of set qualifications for particular offices we have lists of stereotypical virtues and vices used to indicate in general terms the character of ecclesiastical leaders. Furthermore, most of the virtues are not distinctively Christian but are those recognized by society at large. Some commentators have illustrated the public nature of these virtues by showing how similar they are to qualifications for Roman generals.[44] The purpose of these lists of qualifications is to ensure the social respectability of leaders in the church.

The most important qualification is a good reputation in society. For example, the bishop "must be well thought of by outsiders, or he may fall into reproach."[45] By their conduct widows must "give the opponent no opportunity to revile us."[46] Leaders must be without blame,[47] and hospitable to outsiders.[48] Twice the author requires bishops to be *sōphrōn,* or "moderate," and in both instances the word clearly implies social prudence, or *savoir faire.*[49] Likewise, he requires bishops, deacons, and the wives of deacons to be *semnos,* or "dignified,"[50] which one scholar has explained as "the manner of living which honors the rules [*Ordnungen*] of society."[51]

This idealization of church leaders stands in stark contrast to the Paul of the legend tradition. Nothing in the legends suggests that Paul or any other Christian could be characterized as moderate or dignified; rather, they are proudly presented as socially deviant, impudent, and incorrigible. Against this background it appears that the author of the Pastoral

Epistles wanted to replace the obstreperous prophet with the obsequious bishop.

Nowhere is this emphasis on social respectability more in conflict with the legends than in the requirement that every leader have demonstrated dedication to and competence in leading the *oikia,* or household. In fact, the most concrete requirement for those holding any office is the demand that they be "the husband of one wife" (bishops in 1 Tim. 3:2; presbyters in Titus 1:6; deacons in 1 Tim. 3:12), or in the case of widows, "the wife of one husband" (1 Tim. 5:9). Most interpretations of this requirement focus on the word "one" and therefore claim that the author is primarily opposing second marriages, but in the light of his opposition to celibacy it would seem that the author intended this requirement to exclude not only the twice married but also the never married. This interpretation is consistent with other requirements for the offices. For example, the bishop must "manage his own household well, keeping his children submissive and respectful in every way; for if someone does not know how to manage his own household, how can he care for God's church?" (1 Tim. 3:4–5). A presbyter too must be "the husband of one wife, having children who are believers, and who are not under judgment for debauchery or insubordination" (Titus 1:6). Deacons must be "the husband of one wife, managing well their children and their households" (1 Tim. 3:12). According to the author, women in the order of widows must in fact be widows—not virgins pledged to celibacy—and they must have proven themselves capable in raising children (1 Tim. 5:10). Whereas the legends pit the household and the church against each other as competing social institutions, the Pastorals identify the strength of the church with that of the household. Irresponsibility to one's family is worse than apostasy.[52]

This concern for the welfare of the household also lies behind the author's arguments against teachers who told slaves they had a right to expect manumission from their Christian masters:

> Let all who are under the yoke of slavery regard their masters as worthy of all honor, so that the name of God and the teaching may not be defamed. Those who have believing masters must not be disrespectful on the ground that they are brethren; rather they must serve all the better since those who benefit by their service are believers and beloved.
>
> Teach and urge these duties. If any one teaches otherwise and does not agree with the sound words of our Lord Jesus Christ and the teaching which accords with godliness, he is puffed up with conceit, he knows nothing; he has a morbid craving for controversy and for disputes about words, which

produce envy, dissension, slander, base suspicions, and wrangling among men who are depraved in mind and bereft of the truth. (1 Tim. 6:1–5a)

Titus 2:9 also requires slaves to be submissive to their masters. By reading these two passages together we can reconstruct the events behind the author's objections.

Some slaves were despising and disobeying their masters. They believed that since they were fellow believers, they should no longer be slaves (1 Tim. 6:2; cf. Titus 2:10).[53] Disillusioned and in great pain, some slaves had even abandoned the faith (1 Tim. 6:9–10). As a result of this conflict, the teaching of the church was maligned (1 Tim. 6:1; cf. Titus 2:10), and churches themselves were in turmoil (1 Tim. 6:4–5a).

The author opposes those teachers by calling them arrogant, ignorant, and simply interested in causing disturbances (1 Tim. 6:3–5). Slaves who heed them are using piety as a means of financial advantage in a thirst for wealth (vs. 6–9), but piety has advantage only when it is accompanied by stoiclike contentment with nothing more than food and clothing—the minimal provisions for a slave (v. 8).[54] Therefore, slaves must not treat their masters with envy or contempt but with respect, obedience, and good faith, serving them all the better since they are fellow believers (vs. 1–2; Titus 2:9–10).

Similarly, Ignatius counsels Polycarp to refuse the requests of slaves that the church provide payments for their manumission, lest they become "slaves of lust."[55] The repeated statements in Christian documents from Asia Minor that slaves remain in subjection suggests that these churches were indeed embroiled in controversies over slavery—with the legends and the Pastoral Epistles on opposing sides and both appealing to the authority of Paul.[56]

Thus far we have seen how the author used his depictions of the false teachers, of the dying Paul, of Timothy and Titus, and of bishops, presbyters, and deacons to dissociate Paul from his legendary memory. But it is also possible to show that he attempted to silence the storytellers by restricting the influence of the order of widows.

Silencing the Storytellers

From 1 Tim. 5:3–16 it is clear that the institution of widows was thriving in the communities from which the Pastoral Epistles came. Women in the order included the young as well as the old;[57] they had pledged themselves to celibacy;[58] they were supported by the community at large;[59] and they were responsible for intercessory prayer, acts of mercy, and visitation.[60] The church in Smyrna also supported the order of widows, which included some women who had never married.[61] Apparently, the order presented Polycarp with some difficulties. Ignatius commands him: "Do not let the widows be neglected. After the Lord, you yourself be their manager. Let nothing be done without your approval" (Ignatius, *Polycarp* 4:1). Some have understood this passage to mean that Polycarp must care for the widows' material needs, but from other passages it would appear that Polycarp must keep the widows under control. In other words, make sure *widows* do nothing "without your approval." In his letter to the Philippians, Polycarp sets standards for widows and virgins lest they cause the community to be scorned by outsiders, and among these standards are warnings against slander and lying (Polycarp, *Philippians* 4:3; 5:3). No one is permitted to boast about continence (Ignatius, *Polycarp* 5:2), and widows must not encourage other women to leave their husbands for the sake of pursuing celibacy. Presumably, this is why Ignatius commands Polycarp: "Speak to my sisters that they may love the Lord, and be content with their husbands in flesh and spirit" (Ignatius, *Polycarp* 5:1; cf. Polycarp, *Philippians* 4:2).

The author of the Pastoral Epistles also had problems with the order of widows, and he wanted to decimate the office by denying eligibility to any woman under sixty years of age, to any whose character was questionable, and to any who could have found support from relatives or friends.[62]

The author gives three reasons for his limitations of the order: (1) the church is financially burdened; (2) some of the younger widows have broken their pledges to celibacy; and (3) some of the widows are going from house to house saying things they should not. When one examines each of these objections individually, it appears that the author's primary objection was to their itinerant communication.

1. Three times—once at the beginning, once at the end, and once in the middle—we find almost identical formulas, each of which commands families and friends to assume the economic care of the widows:

> If a widow has children or grandchildren, let them first learn their religious duty to their own family and make some return to their parents; for this is acceptable in the sight of God. (1 Tim. 5:4; the "religious duty" probably refers to the Fifth Commandment, Ex. 20:12)

> If any one does not provide for his relatives, and especially for his own family, he has disowned the faith and is worse than an unbeliever. (V. 8)

> If any believing woman has widows, let her assist them; let not the church be burdened, so that it may assist those who are true widows. (V. 16)

It would appear that members of the community were not caring for the widows in their own families and were expecting the community at large to do so. The most natural reading of v. 16 is to take the "believing woman" who "has widows" as a woman who kept widows in her home and who received financial assistance for doing so from the church. Without doubt, such houses for widows were common in early Christian communities.[63]

In spite of the request that the church be relieved of financial responsibility for the widows, it is unlikely that the author's primary objection to the order was economic. Notice that only in v. 16 is it stated that the church's budget was burdened. In the first two passages the motivation is not economic but religious: it is a "religious duty" to provide for one's own (v. 4); one has "disowned the faith and is worse than an unbeliever" if he or she does not provide for relatives (v. 8). Furthermore, it would appear that the communities addressed in the Pastoral Epistles were relatively well-to-do. Rich people and slave owners who profited from the work of their believing slaves were members of the community (1 Tim. 6:1–11, 17–19). Notice also that immediately after this passage on widows—with its alleged concern for the budget—we find:

> Let the elders who rule well be considered worthy of double pay *(diplēs timēs)*, especially those who labor in preaching and teaching; for the scripture says, "You shall not muzzle an ox when it is treading out the grain," and, "The laborer deserves his wages." (1 Tim. 5:17–18)

The author would pay the elders double and the widows less. We must probe deeper than economics if we are to understand why the widows were considered a liability.

2. Apparently some younger widows who had made pledges of chastity to Christ had later desired to marry, and therefore, in the author's opinion, had incurred judgment (1 Tim. 5:11–12). His objection is not to the marriage as such—which he himself commends to the younger widows—but to the violation of the vow. No doubt this was a problem for the widows, as it has been for many ascetic orders, whether ancient or modern, male or female. Nonetheless, there is more to his objection than appears at first sight.

Notice that the author does not say the young widows desire to *re*marry; it simply says to marry (vs. 12 and 14). Furthermore, the author several times prohibits second marriages; in fact, in this very context he writes that the widow must have been the wife of only one husband (v. 9). This would suggest that these young widows were not actually widows at all, but were like the virgin-widows known to Ignatius and Tertullian.[64] Surely this was the case. The author says the community should support only "true widows" *(hai ontōs chērai)*, which almost all commentators have taken to mean those women in the order in contrast to other widows in the congregation. This interpretation would seem well girded by v. 16, which reads: "If some believing woman has widows, let her care for them, and do not let the church be burdened, in order that it might care for the true widows." But it is also possible to take the "true widow" as one who in fact was a widow, in contrast to an unmarried woman enrolled in the order. In support of this interpretation is not only the author's command that young widows marry, even though he objects to *re*marriage, but also his insistence that the true widow is one who has been left alone *(hē de ontōs chēra kai memonōmenē, v. 5)*. Furthermore, the true widow must have demonstrated her abilities in child rearing and in domestic hospitality (v. 10). It would appear then that the reference to the "true widows" in v. 16 is not primarily intended to distinguish between those in the order of widows and the other widows in the community, but to reaffirm that only women who have in fact been widowed are eligible for support. In any case, this breach of the pledge by young widows probably was not the author's primary objection to the order, because it does not account for his insistence that even the older widows be taken from the roll if they can find other support.

3. The author complains that some widows "also learn to be idle when they make housecalls, and not only to be idle, but also to be trivia peddlers *(phlyaroi)* and busybodies, speaking what is not acceptable" *(lalousai ta mē deonta, v. 13)*. Perhaps here we find the author's deepest irritations with the widows. At least it would account for the polymorphous limitations he placed on the enrollment. Some of the widows in their housecalls have been transmitters of communications objectionable to our author. Unfortunately, we are not told the content of any communication, but surely it was not heresy—say, Gnostic or Marcionite—or the author certainly would have raised this objection and excluded them not only from the order of widows but from the fellowship as well, since that is frequently his solution for theological disagreements.[65]

If the general thesis of this book has been correct—namely, that the Pastoral Epistles were written to contradict the image of Paul in popular legends—and if the legends were told by women to justify their celibate ministries, it would not be mere conjecture to think that the communication referred to in 1 Timothy 5 included such legends as these. Confirmation of this interpretation comes from other passages in the Pastorals.

In Titus 2:3b–5 the author says that if women are to teach at all, they must "teach what is good, and so train the young women to love their husbands and children, to be sensible, chaste, domestic, kind, and submissive to their husbands, that the word of God may not be discredited." Presumably, the widows in their housecalls had taught the opposite: they taught celibacy and not domestication, independence and not submission. As we have seen in our discussion of the false teachers, there seems to be a relationship between "the profane tales told by old women" and the rejection of marriage. The author of the Pastorals clearly assumes that the Christian message would be discredited if women were not submissive to their husbands. Over and over again in the legends we are told that a primary source of antagonism against the church was the refusal of women to comply with the desires of their husbands and lovers. It would appear that the author of the Pastorals wanted to soften such tensions by insisting on the domestication of women and by silencing them.

Nowhere is the relationship between silencing women and returning them to diapers and aprons more apparent than in 1 Tim. 2:11–15, where Paul tells women to be silent, submissive, and domestic, for their very salvation depends on their bearing children and bringing them up in the faith.

It is reasonable to conclude that the author of the Pastoral Epistles had two primary purposes in disguising his letters in Pauline garb. First, he wanted to show that the socially radical Paul of the legends was a distortion. Even on the eve of his execution Paul bears no animus for Rome, encourages a conciliatory posture toward society, and emphasizes the value of the household for the success of the church. Second, he wanted to silence those who were telling the stories. In order to do this he forbade women to teach—except to teach younger women how to be content and efficient housewives—he decimated the order of widows, and scorned their stories as so many "old wives' tales."[66] In the following chapter we shall see how effectively the author's Pauline mask disguised his intentions and allowed the Pastoral Epistles to take their present place in the New Testament.

CHAPTER IV

The Victory
of the Pastoral Epistles

The author of the Pastoral Epistles succeeded in passing off his letters as if they came from Paul's own hand. In part this success was due to his brilliant use of the pseudonymous epistle, but perhaps even more important was the social situation in Asia Minor in the mid and late second century. The acceptance of the epistles and the rejection of the *Acts of Paul* must be seen in the light of the struggles in the church between the forces fighting for the older socially radical sectarianism and those struggling for the social legitimation of the church.

The author was not idiosyncratic in his conservative orientation, but stood within a long-standing literary tradition which tried to domesticate the apocalyptic radicalism of the church. This tradition affirmed the imminent return of Christ but refused to associate this hope with socially radical behavior. For example, the author of Colossians writes that Christians should make the most of the present time before the end by behaving "wisely toward outsiders" (Col. 4:5). Likewise, the author of 1 Peter writes: "The end of all things is at hand; therefore keep sane and sober" (1 Peter 4:7). And again: "Maintain good conduct among the Gentiles, so that in case they speak against you as wrongdoers, they may see your good deeds and glorify God on the day of visitation" (2:12). 1 Peter then continues by explicating what these good deeds should include: Christians must be subject to every human institution, slaves must stay in servitude, wives must be submissive, and all must honor the emperor (2:13, 17, 18; 3:1).[1]

Ignatius, Polycarp, and the Pastoral Epistles share this orientation. They indicate that the time before the Parousia is short (e.g., Ignatius, *Ephesians* 11:1; *Polycarp* 3:2; 1 Tim. 4:1; and 2 Tim. 3:1), while consistently tempering the radicalism of their fellow believers. Even Ignatius, who claimed that the greatness of Christianity lay not in its persuasiveness but in its being hated by the world (Ignatius, *Romans* 3:3), wrote that Christians should not haggle with each other "lest God's throng be blasphemed because of a few fools" (Ignatius, *Trallians* 8:2). Once again we see that one source of social conflict was the disruption of the household, for he tells the Ephesians: "Do not err, my brethren; they who corrupt families shall not inherit the kingdom of God" (Ignatius, *Ephesians* 16:1). Ignatius' letters leave little doubt that most bishops in Asia Minor wanted to make the church more socially acceptable.[2]

The bishops' ameliorating posture no doubt contributed to the rapid growth of the church. Those coming into the church were no longer expected to follow the rigorous and sometimes peculiar practices of earlier apocalyptic communities. By consolidating their authority the bishops provided a more continuous, uniform, and reciprocal structure for leadership from city to city. All evidence of Christianity in second-century Asia Minor witnesses to vitality and growth.

But to some Christians in Asia Minor the softening of the boundaries between the church and outsiders appeared to be nothing less than compromise with the world. Dissatisfaction with the accommodation of the church to the standards of the macrosociety provided a seedbed for a new outcropping of Christian radicalism at the beginning of the latter half of the second century. Under the emperors Antoninus Pius and Marcus Aurelius, Asia Minor experienced a series of persecutions, and among the martyrs was the immensely popular bishop Polycarp (d. 156). During the same period the worst plague in antiquity devastated Asia Minor. The combination of this political and physical adversity fanned the old but never dead coals of apocalypticism, and once again the fires of religious fanaticism spread throughout the subcontinent.

THE RESURGENCE OF APOCALYPTIC RADICALISM

The fires began in Phrygia during the sixth decade of the second century with the activity of several prophets in a movement originally known as the "New Prophecy" or—to its detractors—the "Phrygian Sect." In order to designate the movement as the brainchild of a single heresiarch, writers in the fourth century called it "Montanism" after Montanus, the most influential of the prophets.[3] But Montanism was not a personality cult: Montanus was merely *primus inter pares* with other prophets, such as Alcibiades, Miltiades, Themiso, Theodotus, and the prophetesses Maximilla and Priscilla.

Montanists considered their prophecies to be the "last gifts" *(eschata charismata);* that is, this outpouring of the Spirit indicated that the Parousia, the Judgment, and the millennial reign of Christ were imminent So impassioned was this expectation of the end that certain

Montanist prophets encouraged the faithful to sell their goods and to travel together to the expected site of the Parousia. Montanists required all Christians to reject this world which was so soon to be destroyed. Those who participated in the imperial cult or who in other ways compromised the faith were severely disciplined.[4] Martyrdom became a desirable fate: "Do not hope to die in bed or in abortion or in languishing fevers, but in martyrdom; that he who suffered for you may be glorified."[5]

Consistent with this ethical rigorism was Montanus' annulling of marriages.[6] Priscilla and Maximilla divorced their husbands, and Priscilla thereafter was called a virgin.[7] The prophet Proclus remained a virgin throughout life.[8] They also observed strict diets inasmuch as they believed fasting and eating only dried foods (*xērophagia*) were helpful in preparation for receiving revelation.

Phrygian religion even before the birth of Jesus was notoriously fanatical, and some have suggested that the origin of Montanism is best explained as a mixture of Christianity and local enthusiastic religion. But even if Epiphanius is correct in claiming that Montanus had been a pagan priest, recent research shows clearly that the roots of the movement are embedded firmly in the soil of traditional Asian Christianity. As one authority on Montanism has put it:

> One must not look for the actual point of origin for the rise of Montanism in the Phrygian national character or cults. The demands of the New Prophecy are in fact none other than those recognized generally in the church to correspond with the ideal of Christian perfection. Because the essence of Montanism is properly defined as a reaction—from the perspective of the imminent Parousia and based on a legal link with direct, divine prophetic authority—against the church becoming more worldly, it cannot have its roots in national characteristics, but it is grounded partially in a general perception of Christianity which deviated from genuine [sic] Christian understanding, and partially in the particular situation of the church at the time.[9]

No doubt it was precisely because the New Prophecy traded on popular Christian tradition that it was so successful—and not only in Phrygia. By 180 it had spread to Pontus, Crete, and Gaul, and by the turn of the century to Rome and northern Africa.

The movement seems to have caught the dominant church off balance in that, unlike Gnostics or Marcionites, Montanists were not doctrinal heretics.[10] They interpreted the church's own Scriptures, laid claim to the same prophetic tradition, and rigorously maintained certain high ethical standards better than most Christians. It is easy to see how zealous believers like Tertullian were attracted to the movement. Even Victor, bishop of Rome, at first accepted the movement, recognized the prophecies of Montanus, Priscilla, and Maximilla, and made peace with the churches of Asia and Phrygia.[11]

THE VICTORY OF THE BISHOPS
AND THE FATE OF APOCALYPTIC LITERATURE

Bishops closer to the situation, however, were not so conciliatory. Sometime between 160 and 165 two bishops from southern Phrygia (Zoticus of Cumana and Julian of Apamea) traveled to Pepuza to examine Maximilla's prophecies to see if they were of God.[12] But when they arrived, Themiso and other Montanists who were in control of the church in the city silenced them. Likewise, bishop Sotas of Anchialus, Thrace, convinced that Priscilla possessed a demon, attempted to exorcize her, but was stopped by her followers.[13] Apollinarius, bishop of Hierapolis, disputed with Montanists in Ancyra, Galatia, and was successful in refuting them.[14] The concern of Phrygian and Thracian bishops over the success of the New Prophecy is also clear from a synod held in Hierapolis under Apollinarius—the first known assembly of its kind in the history of the church. Twenty-seven bishops attended and condemned the prophecies of Montanus, Maximilla, and Theodotus. Shortly thereafter twelve bishops met in Anchialus, Thrace, under bishop Sotas for the same purpose.[15]

One must not interpret this opposition of the bishops to the New Prophecy merely as a rejection of false doctrine. Rather, by rejecting Montanism the bishops were struggling to maintain their authority in the church against charismatic leadership. It was bishop against prophet; apostolic succession against prophetic enthusiasm. The bishops justified their office by claiming to be descendants of the apostles through the "laying on of hands" in ordination, while the prophets claimed to be heirs of the Paraclete and the legacy of earlier Christian prophets.

In their opposition to the New Prophecy the bishops produced a substantial literature, such as the books of Apollinarius, Apollonius, Miltiades, Melito, Rhodo, Gaius, and an unknown author called "the Anonymous." From the little that remains of this anti-Montanist literature it is clear that their primary objections were to Montanist deviant behavior—especially their ecstasy—and not to their theology. For example, Apollinarius criticizes Montanus for "disturbing the populace."[16]

On the other hand, Montanists produced their own literature. The-miso sent a "catholic epistle" to various congregations defending the New Prophecy,[17] and Proclus was accused of composing new scriptures.[18] Tertullian owned a book containing oracles from Montanus, which may have been identical to a book known to the Anonymous as *According to Asterius Urbanus.*[19] Apollinarius knew of a Montanist book opposing Miltiades, and responded with one of his own.[20] Many of Tertullian's own writings are in defense of the New Prophecy.

The bishops soon prevailed. In spite of its early popularity, Montanism quickly became a marginal movement. After the first half of the third century it was no longer a serious threat to the church. The Edict of Arcadius in 398 ordered the burning of all Montanist books, and only those written by Tertullian escaped the flames. What is too often overlooked, however, is the similar fate of literature technically not Montanist but from the same apocalyptic, socially radical tradition. As we shall see, some of the bishops rejected or ignored the Apocalypse of John, Papias' *Expositions,* and the *Acts of Paul* because of their congeniality with the New Prophecy.[21]

THE APOCALYPSE OF JOHN

As one would expect, the Apocalypse of John was used primarily by Christians with an apocalyptic orientation: e.g., Papias, Justin Martyr, Montanists, Melito of Sardis, Irenaeus, and Tertullian. Early in the third century, no doubt in reaction to Montanism, several authors challenged the inspiration of the Apocalypse. A presbyter of Rome early in the third century named Gaius, kindred in theology to Zephyrinus and Callistus, bishops of Rome, wrote a refutation of the Montanist Proclus in which he rejects the Apocalypse as the forgery of the heretic Cerinthus.[22] It is quite possible that the now lost *Defense of the Gospel and Apocalypse of John,* written by Hippolytus of Rome, a rigorist and chiliast, was directed against such persons as Gaius.

Gaius was not the only one who rejected the Apocalypse in this period. Dionysius of Alexandria near the middle of the third century wrote two books against Nepos, an Egyptian apocalyptic bishop, in which Dionysius gives us the following clue concerning the sharp criticisms the Apocalypse had been exposed to by anti-apocalyptic Christians:

> Now some before our time have set aside this book, and repudiated it entirely, criticising it chapter by chapter, and endeavouring to show it to be without either sense or reason. They have alleged also that its title is false; for they deny that John is the author. Nay, further, they hold that it can be no sort of revelation, because it is covered with so gross and

dense a veil of ignorance. They affirm, therefore, that none of the apostles, nor indeed any of the saints, nor any person belonging to the Church, could be its author; but that Cerinthus, and the heretical sect founded by him, and named after him the Cerinthian sect, being desirous of attaching the authority of a great name to the fiction propounded by him, prefixed that title to the book. For the doctrine inculcated by Cerinthus is this: that there will be an earthly reign of Christ. ... But I, for my part, could not venture to set this book [the Apocalypse] aside, for there are many brethren who value it highly. Yet, having formed an idea of it as a composition exceeding my capacity of understanding, I regard it as containing a kind of hidden and wonderful intelligence on the several subjects which come under it. For though I cannot comprehend it, I still suspect that there is some deeper sense underlying the words.[23]

Dionysius himself, true to his Origenistic orientation, allegorizes the Apocalypse and thereby is able to keep it, without accepting its apocalypticism. This equivocation is apparent also in the Origenist Eusebius of Caesarea, who says that some Christians placed the book with those of undisputed value, while others placed it among the disputed works.[24] Similarly *Canon Muratori* accepts the Apocalypse but acknowledges that some in Rome "will not have the letter read in the Church." The Synod of Laodicea (ca. 360) did not include the book, and Cyril of Jerusalem (d. 386) adamantly forbade it.

It would appear that the Montanist movement required the church to reevaluate the Apocalypse. Some, like Gaius, rejected it as a literary forgery; some, like Hippolytus, affirmed its apostolicity and apocalypticism; and some, like Dionysius, affirmed the book, but only because they could allegorize its mysteries and thereby mollify its social radicalism.

PAPIAS' *EXPOSITIONS OF THE ORACLES OF THE LORD*

Papias' *Expositions* fared even worse. With the one noteworthy exception of Irenaeus, no author of the early church so much as mentions the five-volume work until Eusebius does so in the fourth century. Nevertheless, it is clear that the *Expositions* had been copied and circulated before that time. Not only did Eusebius have access to a copy, but he thought his readers did as well: "We ... refer our readers to the books themselves."[25] Several authors in the sixth and seventh centuries knew of the books and quoted from them.[26] If copies of the *Expositions* were available, the silence of the church fathers requires some explaining, expecially since it must have been a trove of early Christian lore. An explanation is suggested from a comparison of the two earliest references to the book.

Even though Eusebius gives the *Expositions* a measure of credence, he warns his readers about its "contradictory" *(paradoxos)* and "fictitious" *(mythikos)* contents. In particular, he objects to Papias' claim "that there will be a millennium after the resurrection from the dead, when the personal reign of Christ will be established on this earth."[27] This is precisely the reason which Dionysius of Alexandria gave for the fact that some Christians before him had rejected the Apocalypse of John. It would therefore appear that Eusebius recognized that the chiliasm of the *Expositions*—like that of the Apocalypse—represented a religious mentality uncongenial to the church after the conversion of Constantine to Christ and the conversion of the church to Plato. Surely this uncongeniality lies behind Eusebius' arrogant smear on Papias' abilities: "He was a man of very little intelligence."[28]

Unlike Eusebius, with his superior Greek education and Neo-Platonic philosophy, Irenaeus was schooled in Asia Minor by Papias' friend Polycarp.[29] Therefore, it is no surprise that his use of the *Expositions* reflects only the highest appreciation. Irenaeus himself was a chiliast and moral rigorist, and in his book *Against Heresies* he defends the new revelations of the Spirit in the Phrygian prophets against their detractors.[30] In fact, the church in Lyons, Gaul, over which he became bishop, was strongly influenced by Montanism.[31]

A comparison of the uses of Papias' *Expositions* by Eusebius and Irenaeus indicates that its reception or rejection was largely determined by concerns eschatological, sociological, and ethical. Christians in the second century, influenced by the New Prophecy, persecuted by the authorities, and consciously set apart from the neighbors, were more receptive of the *Expositions* than Christian intellectuals in the fourth century to whom the book must have been an embarrassing reminder of the social radicalism and gullibility which had characterized some earlier believers.

THE ACTS OF PAUL

Perhaps now we can understand the issues involved in the defrocking of the Asian presbyter who wrote the *Acts of Paul*. At first glance, Tertullian's reference to the event seems to suggest that the bishops objected to the use of Paul's name in the title of the book, but the title itself makes no pretense whatever that the book had been written by the apostle. Was the action against the presbyter simply a reaction against pseudepigrapha, or was it influenced by other factors? Would the bishops have dismissed him if they had agreed with the contents of the

Acts of Paul? As we have seen,[32] Lipsius suggested that the presbyter was defrocked because of heresy—i.e., Gnosticism. But now, after the reconstruction of the *Acts of Paul* by Carl Schmidt, it is clear that the author was not a Gnostic.

I suggest that the author was a victim in the conflict between the bishops and the New Prophecy. As far as we can tell, the book was written sometime between 160 and 190, precisely when the conflict was most intense. The chiliasm, social radicalism, and emphasis on prophecy surely would have been unwelcomed by the bishops. Furthermore, it is possible that the Pastorals already were gaining acceptance and were influencing the image of Paul in the church. Regardless, the reactionary opposition to Montanist writings in this period, as well as the criticism of the Apocalypse of John, and the silence regarding Papias' *Expositions* all suggest that the bishops rejected the *Acts of Paul* as much for its eschatology and social values as for its concocted Pauline speeches.

THE VICTORY OF THE PASTORALS
AND THE FATE OF THE PAULINE CORPUS

The process whereby the Pastoral Epistles became almost universally accepted in the dominant church before the beginning of the third century is extremely difficult to reconstruct because of the silence of our sources. The first uncontested quotation from them is in Irenaeus (ca. 190), but without question they were known, read, and circulated before this time. The collection of Paul's letters made by Marcion (ca. 150) does not contain the Pastoral Epistles, but we do not know whether he was ignorant of their existence or whether he knew and rejected them— perhaps because they criticize asceticism and attribute the creation of the world to God.[33] The ascetics Basilides and Tatian (both mid-second century) accepted only Titus, which is silent concerning the issue.[34] The Chester Beatty Papyri (p^{46}; early third century) also lack the Pastorals in the extant remains, but once again their absence may be attributed either to ignorance or to rejection. The papyri come from Egypt, a center of Christian monasticism.

Regardless, by the beginning of the third century the Pastorals took their places alongside the rest of the letters in the Pauline corpus. Frequently the church fathers used them to establish standards for bishops, deacons, and widows (e.g., Clement of Alexandria, Tertullian, Origen, and Cyprian), and to oppose Gnosticism and other traditions forbidding marriages and restricting diets (e.g., Irenaeus, Clement, Origen, and Hippolytus).

According to Tertullian, if he can be trusted as a representative of the New Prophecy in this period, even Montanists accepted the Pastorals. However, in his books *On Monogamy* and *On Fasting*, written after his conversion to Montanism, Tertullian reveals that anti-Montanists were using 1 Tim. 4:1–3 to censure Montanist restrictions on sex and food. In his response Tertullian claimed—wrongly!—that Montanists never forbade marriages but only second marriages.[35] Likewise, he argued that the apostle's condemnation of those who prohibit eating certain foods cannot be applied to Montanists, because they did not reject these foods permanently but only during periods of fasting.[36] By such casuistic sleight of hand Montanists apparently were able to claim the Pastorals as their own and deflect the objections raised by their opponents.

Moreover, by analyzing how Paul's own letters were edited, scholars have found additional evidence of the popularity of the Pastorals. The text of the Pauline letters that lies behind all the extant manuscripts bears signs of harmonization with the Pastorals. That is, all extant manuscripts of the corpus contain interpolations from a scribe who knew the Pastorals and who altered the text of Paul's own letters to conform with them. I shall call this text the archetype, but by this I do not mean that every variant in the corpus ultimately is a deviation from this one text. There probably never was an archetypal text in this sense. Rather, I mean that, for whatever reason, no manuscript omits these interpolations which crept in after the Pastorals were added to the collection.

By detecting a corrupt reading in 1 Cor. 4:6, John Strugnell has shown that the archetype of this passage is at least two stages removed from the original, or autograph.[37] In a recent article entitled "A Conjectural Emendation of 1 Cor. 15:31–32: Or the Case of the Misplaced Lion Fight,"[38] I argue that 1 Cor. 15:31 contains a gloss added by a scribe familiar with the Pastorals. Both alleged corruptions are present in every manuscript of 1 Corinthians, but are never cited by ecclesiastical authors before the third century. In other words, our best reconstructed text of 1 Corinthians seems to contain secondary additions unattested before the year 200. The same is the case with 1 Cor. 14:33b–36, which also was added by someone who knew the Pastorals. We shall discuss this passage in some detail, but first I should say something about the implications of these textual alterations for reconstructing the history of the Pauline corpus.

Since these interpolations witness to the harmonizing of 1 Corinthians with the Pastorals, it is likely that the Pastorals already by this time had been added to the collection. It is also likely that at this stage in the textual tradition the copying of 1 Corinthians was not done separately but in conjunction with the copying of the entire corpus, and if so, other letters may have been shaped by the same concerns. 1 Corinthians is, after all, not the only Pauline letter in which scholars have detected interpolations in the archetype. For example, even though we know that Romans circulated in more than one edition—both with and without chs. 15 and 16—all manuscripts now contain these chapters. Because our present manuscripts do not reflect the variety of forms in which these letters were known in the early church, the parent text behind these manuscripts itself is a selective text, and probably derivative.

By analyzing the interpolation between 1 Cor. 14:33a and 37 we can see one of the concerns that informed the editing of our archetype. The interpolation appears below in parallel columns, with its equivalent in 1 Timothy 2.

1 Cor. 14:33b–36　　　　　　　　　　　　　　1 Tim. 2:11–13

As in all the churches of the saints,
let women keep silent in the churches. ———— Let a woman learn in silence in all
　　　　　　　　　　　　　　　　　—subordination *(hypotagē)*.
For they are not permitted *(epitrepetai)*———— And I do not permit *(epitrepō)*
to speak,　　　　　　　　　　　　　　　a woman to teach or to have authority
　　　　　　　　　　　　　　　　　over a man, but to be in silence.
but let them be subordinate *(hypotassesthōsan)*
as even the law says.———————————— For Adam was formed first, then Eve.
And if they desire to learn something let
them ask their own husbands at home. For it
is shameful for a woman to speak in church.
What! Did the word of God originate with
you, or are you the only ones it has reached?

The interpolation seems to contradict 1 Cor. 11:3–16 and the general tone of chs. 12 and 14 where Paul assumes that women will speak in church. Moreover, because the interpolation interrupts the flow of ch. 14, some texts relocate vs. 33 and 34 to the end of the chapter to make it read more smoothly.[39]

What can we say about the interpolator from this passage? He was male, literate, had access to a copy of 1 Corinthians, 1 Timothy, and perhaps to all of the letters in the corpus. By his reference to "all the churches of the saints" and his statement that the Corinthian practice deviated from other communities the interpolator reveals his ecumenical consciousness. Furthermore, he considers the household—not the church—the context for women speaking and learning. They are to learn from their husbands, which indicates that the author both condoned marriage, and left little opportunity for the education of unwed women. When he claims that it is shameful for women to speak in church he is not arguing theologically or philosophically. His argument, like many of those in the Pastorals, is simply that such behavior violates dominant social conventions. Thus he seems less concerned about disruptions in worship than about disruptions in society.

We can also learn something about our scribe by assessing the location of the interpolation. Of course, it is natural that he would have inserted it into 1 Corinthians, inasmuch as it is the only letter in which we find women speaking at all. In 1 Cor. 11:3–16, Paul says that when women pray or prophesy they must keep their veils on. Notice that he does not forbid them to pray and prophesy. But if the scribe wanted to silence women, why did he put the interpolation in ch. 14 and not here in ch. 11? I suggest that the women he wanted to silence were prophetesses, and ch. 14 is the only place in the entire Pauline corpus where the apostle establishes guidelines for prophets. By analyzing the verses immediately preceding the interpolation we can see that the issue for the scribe was not women chattering in the back row but women speaking in the Spirit:

> Let two or three prophets speak, and let the others weigh what is said. If a revelation is made to another sitting by, let the first be silent. For you can all prophesy one by one, so that all may learn and all be encouraged; and the spirits of prophets are subject to prophets. For God is not a God of confusion but of peace. (1 Cor. 14:29–33a)

The section immediately following the interpolation is even more revealing of its intention, inasmuch as here the apostle requires that those who presume to be prophets recognize that his instructions are from God. Originally Paul's claim of divine instruction would have followed his suggestion that prophets speak one after the other, but in the interpolated version it follows the disavowal of prophetesses.

> If any one thinks that he is a prophet, or spiritual *(pneumati-kos)*, he should acknowledge that what I am writing to you is a command of the Lord. If any one does not recognize this, he is not recognized. So, my brethren, earnestly desire to prophesy. (1 Cor. 14:37–39a)

Clearly, the scribe restricts this desire to prophesy to men, and excludes such persons as the daughters of Philip, the prophetess "Jezebel" of Thyatira, and Ammia of Philadelphia, who prophesied early in the second century. The scribe may even have been thinking of the Montanist prophetesses. In any case, the interpolation resonates with the denunciations of prophetesses by anti-Montanist bishops.

In no way do I intend to say that the primary motivation for the creation of our archetypal text of the Pauline letters was to silence women. Obviously, the primary motivation was the desire to preserve and distribute the apostle's letters for the nurture of the church. In fact, I would claim that the interpolator probably thought that by harmonizing 1 Corinthians with the Pastoral Epistles he was only explaining an obscure Pauline text by a clearer one.[40] Furthermore, the scribe did not expunge from his text passages potentially embarrassing to socially conservative Christians in the second century. His tendency seems to have been to gloss—not to delete—and all in the service of the gospel.

But it is clear that the Pauline corpus as we now know it represents the work of only one line of the Pauline legacy, a line characterized by literate men, ecumenically aware, aligned with the developing episcopacy, and in some cases opposed to prophetesses and to storytelling women who remembered Paul as a fanatical, marginal social type.

In other words, the Pauline corpus has not come down to us with the accuracy and dispassion of a genderless Xerox machine. It has come down to us from the hands of pious, dedicated, and skilled men—males of a particular social position and world view, who, in spite of their respect for the Pauline text, put their own signatures to his letters, and thereby to some extent helped him write them. The Pauline corpus is mostly his, but also unmistakably theirs.

It therefore would appear that by the end of the second century the Pastoral Epistles had won the literary battle for Paul's memory: not only had they made their way into the Pauline corpus, they had influenced the transmission of Paul's authentic writings. Now Paul was sufficiently domesticated to serve the needs of a church increasingly eager to gain social acceptability.

CHAPTER V

The Victory
of the Legends

Thus far it might appear that the Pastoral Epistles were the only victors in the battle for Paul's memory, but matters were much more complex. Even though the presbyter who wrote the *Acts of Paul* was removed from his office, his book continued to be read in some circles. No less a sophisticated theologian than Origen quoted from it favorably,[1] Manichaeans used it as scripture,[2] and the author of Codex Claromontanus (fourth century) had before him a biblical manuscript that contained it.[3] Furthermore, two sections of the *Acts of Paul* circulated independently at an early date and long enjoyed popularity. The *Acts of Paul and Thecla* has come down to us in Greek, Coptic, Syriac, Slavic, Arabic, and four independent Latin versions.[4] In Syria it was added to the books of Ruth, Esther, Judith, and Susanna to comprise the "Book of Women."[5] As late as the seventh century an ecclesiastical official had to remind the church to exclude the *Acts of Paul and Thecla* from its scriptures.[6] The *Martyrdom of Paul* (=AP 11) was read on the day commemorating Paul's death and thus was widely used.[7] Early in the textual transmission, no doubt because of its popularity, the text of the *Martyrdom* "ran wild."[8] Considerable deviations exist between the shorter version of the story, preserved in Greek, Coptic, Syriac, Latin, and Ethiopic, on the one hand, and its longer version preserved in four families of Latin manuscripts on the other.[9] But the primary victory of the legends lies outside literary circles.

Even though the Pastorals made their way into the New Testament and influenced the editing of the Pauline corpus, they did not halt the transmission of the legends. The oral tradition, precisely because it was oral,[10] was little affected by the literary activity that produced the New Testament. The Pastorals were canonized as genuinely Pauline because they persuaded the minds of the intellectuals, but Thecla was canonized as a saint because she won the hearts of the pious, especially in Asia Minor. Thecla was a victor in her own way.

In about the year 300, Methodius, bishop of Olympus and Patara, both in Lycia (southwest Asia Minor), wrote a *Symposium* modeled after that of Plato, only instead of men philosophizing about love *(erōs)*, ten virgins praise virtue *(aretē)*. Each virgin argues that chastity is the pinnacle of virtue, but none does so more articulately than Thecla. After hearing each of the speeches, Lady Virtue herself, Arete, pronounces Thecla the winner,[11] and in celebration Thecla leads the other virgins in an antiphonal hymn in which she sings of her experiences:

> Leaving marriage and the beds of mortals and my golden home for Thee, O King, I have come in undefiled robes, in order that I might enter within Thy happy bridal chamber. . . . Having escaped, O blessed One, from the innumerable enchanting wiles of the serpents, and, moreover, from the flames of fire, and from the mortal-destroying assaults of wild beasts, I await Thee from heaven. . . . I forget my own country, O Lord, through desire of Thy grace. I forget also the company of virgins, my fellows, the desire even of mother and of kindred, for Thou, O Christ, art all things to me.[12]

It is impossible to determine with certainty if Methodius knew of the story from the *Acts of Paul* or from oral tradition or from both; nevertheless, it is clear that he presumed it was well known and venerated by his readers.

In the year 327 c.e. a woman named Emmelia in Caesarea of Cappadocia was told in a dream that she would have a daughter whom she should name Thecla, after "that Thecla whose fame is great among the virgins," probably meaning that the saint enjoyed popularity among the virgins of the area.[13] The girl born was indeed named Macrina Thecla, the elder virgin sister of Basil the Great and Gregory of Nyssa. Her brother Gregory and his friend Gregory of Nazianzus, both from Cappadocia, wrote of the legendary Thecla as a model of virginity and martyrdom.[14] Their younger contemporary, Theodore of Mopsuestia, in Cilicia, wrote an oration to her,[15] and Athanasius wrote a *Life of St. Thecla.*[16]

Confirmation of Thecla's continued popularity among women comes from a sermon of John Chrysostom delivered late in the fourth century in which he scolds the women of Constantinople for applauding Thecla's sacrifices but dressing themselves in luxuriant garments.[17] Chrysostom himself was a champion of the celibate life, having been a hermit under the Pachomian Rule for eight years, and a supporter of the orders of virgins and widows that flourished there.[18] Constantinople became a center for the veneration of Thecla. Early in the sixth century the emperor Justinian built a church there in her honor, and within two centuries two more churches were erected to her.[19]

But throughout Asia Minor her name was invoked over monasteries and in inscriptions.[20] An early-sixth-century ivory case, probably from Anatolia, beautifully portrays Paul preaching to Thecla, who listens from the wall of Iconium.[21] In memory of the virgin many Christian women in Asia Minor were given her name,[22] among whom was a woman to whom Gregory of Nazianzus wrote four letters, and who probably was the head of a convent.[23]

Nowhere was Thecla more popular than in Seleucia of Isauria on the coast of southern Asia Minor, where, according to the *Acts of Paul* and tradition, she settled after leaving Paul. Gregory of Nazianzus, who lived in Seleucia for some time, called it "the city of the holy and illustrious virgin Thecla,[24] and wrote of the convent there dedicated to her. The altar sat over the cave where tradition says the earth swallowed her up to prevent her from being defiled by doctors who were jealous of her healing miracles and who tried to rape her. Archaeologists have discovered the site of this convent near a little village south of Seleucia, sometimes called Becili, or Meriamlik, or Ayatekla (=Hagia-Thekla).[25] They found a richly decorated, huge basilica—over eighty meters long—dedicated to the saint. The church dates from 460–470 c.e., but bears signs of an earlier, simpler form. The sheer size and splendor of the structure attest to the vitality of the cult. Thecla was a new Athena, and her sanctuary was a new Parthenon. Later in the fifth century the emperor Zeno, a native Isaurian, built another church to Thecla nearby the great basilica. It was considerably smaller, but magnificently designed. In the Middle Ages another church was built inside the cave where Thecla allegedly had died.

Sometime in the fifth century a resident of Seleucia, perhaps bishop Basil of Seleucia, wrote a two-volume work entitled the *Life and Miracles of Saint Thecla.*[26] The first volume is simply a literary paraphrase of the story in the *Acts of Paul and Thecla,* which by this time had already circulated independently. The second volume is a series of forty-six miracles attributed to Thecla by Christians in the area, which provides us with a window through which to see entire provinces of Asia Minor devoted to the worship of this virgin-martyr. In addition to the shrine at Seleucia we discover references to shrines to Thecla at Mt. Kokysion (mir. 2), at Aigai in Cilicia (mirs. ̊ and 39), and at Dalisandos, whose exact location is not known, but apparently was not far from Seleucia. The citizens of Dalisandos frequently held panegyrics in honor of the virgin which attracted multitudes who climbed a mountain to see Thecla fly by on a chariot of fire (mir. 26).

But Seleucia clearly was the center of the cult. Worshipers came from all over Isauria, Cilicia, and Cyprus, and as far away as Spain and Syria. A fourth-century Spanish nun named Egeria (or Etheria) made a pilgrimage to the Holy Land and on her return visited Thecla's shrine in Seleucia. Fortunately, she kept good notes of her travels, and this is what she says about her visit to the church of St. Thecla:

> On the third day I arrived at a city called Seleucia of Isauria, and, when I got there, I called on the bishop, a very godly man who had been a monk, and saw a very beautiful church in the city. Holy Thecla's is on a small hill about a mile and a half from the city, so, as I had to stay somewhere, it was best to get straight on and spend the night there.
>
> Round the holy church there is a tremendous number of cells for men and women. And that was where I found one of my dearest friends, a holy deaconess called Marthana. I had come to know her in Jerusalem when she was up there on pilgrimage. She was the superior of some cells of apotactites or virgins, and I simply cannot tell you how pleased we were to see each other again. But I must get back to the point.
>
> There are a great many cells on that hill, and in the middle a great wall round the martyrium itself, which is very beautiful. . . . In God's name I arrived at the martyrium, and we had a prayer there, and read the whole Acts of holy Thecla; and I gave heartfelt thanks to God for his mercy in letting me fulfill all my desires so completely, despite all my unworthiness. For two days I stayed there, visiting all the holy monks and apotactites, the men as well as the women; then, after praying and receiving Communion, I went back to Tarsus to rejoin my route.[27]

Egeria was not the only pilgrim who visited the shrine. In about the year 400 the Syrian virgins Marana and Cyra walked, without eating, over two hundred miles to the convent.[28] Not all came to worship. One miracle recorded in the *Life and Miracles of St. Thecla* concerns two men who came from Eirenopolis, Isauria, some forty miles away to attend the festival apparently just to see the many virgins there (mir. 34; cf. mir. 33). They found a virgin walking outside the temple precincts, tried to get her drunk and seduce her, until Thecla appeared to them and rescued her.

Without question, the Thecla cult held a special attraction for women.[29] The author of the *Life and Miracles of St. Thecla* records some fifteen miracles Thecla performed for women[30] and complains that he does not

have the time to list the many other women who were helped by her
(mir. 44). As one authority has said of the depiction of women at
Thecla's temple:

> The women formed a separate society. . . . A woman is rarely
> alone in *Miracles:* Xenarchis is surrounded by women (mir.
> 45); the wetnurse of miracle 24 talks with the other women;
> the ascetics of Hagia-Thekla formed a distinct "choir." There
> existed a feminine solidarity which touches the deep meaning
> of the legend of Thecla.[31]

One story is sufficient to illustrate the importance of the Thecla cult
among women. Sosanna, an esteemed virgin of the temple, told the
author a story about a woman named Dionysia who renounced "her
husband and children and house" *(oikia),* in order to join herself to the
temple. Her first night there Thecla appeared to her. Dionysia was so
changed by that vision that thereafter she became an object of admira-
tion among women for her chastity. Her daughter, also named Dionysia
(her name indicates that she probably was born before her mother's
conversion), followed her mother's example and remained a virgin for
life (mir. 46). In the fifth century as in the second, women told stories
about Thecla encouraging women to leave their families for the sake of
chastity.

No doubt stories like this circulated widely; as the author says: "The
number of Thecla's miracles is innumerable. . . . All peoples, all races, all
cities, all towns, all hamlets, all homes beseech the martyr" (mir. 10; cf.
mir. 18). Stories about Thecla not only permeated Seleucia and Cyprus
(mirs. 15 and 23) but extended far to the east and in the west as far as
provincial Asia (mir. 28).

Modern research on the Thecla cult has shown that the author was
conservative in his estimation of Thecla's acclaim: she was venerated
from the shores of the Caspian almost to the shores of the Atlantic. In
the fourth century a church in Antioch of Syria was dedicated to
Thecla.[32] Another church, in Eschamiadzin, Iberia, from the fifth
century has a wall design showing Paul preaching to her.[33] In Egypt
archaeologists have found depictions of Thecla and wild beasts on two
flasks for holy oil,[34] a fresco of Paul and Thecla on the vault of a
chapel,[35] an ivory bas-relief showing Thecla and Theocleia listening to
Paul from the windows of their home,[36] and an inscription invoking the
virgin-saint.[37] In Rome, scholars found a sarcophagus graced by a relief
portraying Paul and Thecla traveling together in a boat.[38] Jerome in
Jerusalem, Ambrose in Rome, and Sulpicius Severus in Gaul all praise
Thecla as a model of feminine chastity.[39] The *Acts of Xanthippe and*

Polyxena is about women in Spain who hear Paul preach and leave their husbands to follow him. Here again we find a reference to Thecla, as though all the readers would know who she was.[40]

Prosopography documents Thecla's popularity in yet another way. The name Thecla was uncommon in antiquity, except among Christian women, and was especially common among virgins. As might be expected, most of the evidence for the name comes from Asia Minor,[41] but the name is also attested throughout the empire. A third-century virgin in Sicily bore her name,[42] and Jerome tells us of a Roman woman named Melania who acquired the name Thecla because of her continence.[43] In the east, Thecla's namesakes include a Palestinian martyr (d. ca. 304), and two fourth-century Persian martyrs, one of whom was a virgin.[44] An Egyptian virgin named Thecla, a member of an order of celibate women, became a martyr in the Decian persecution (ca. 250), and another of the same name died in 304 in Apollinopolis Parva, Egypt.[45] In the year 300 C.E., a woman named Thecla was executed in Adrumetum, Africa.[46] Inscriptions in Syria and Egypt also attest to the name.[47] Ironically, the second oldest complete text of the Pastoral Epistles appears in Codex Alexandrinus, written by a fourth-century Egyptian woman named Thecla, and apparently an ascetic.[48] Little did she realize that the documents she was copying were written to oppose the legends about her ancient namesake.

Not everyone in the early church failed to recognize the conflict between the Thecla tradition and the Pastorals. We have a record of one debate in which the great popularity of Thecla was used to argue against the Pauline authorship of the Pastorals, or at least of those passages which forbid marriage. Augustine accused Manichaeans of teaching "doctrines of demons," inasmuch as they, like the false teachers denounced in 1 Tim. 4:1–3, forbade "people to marry and to eat foods which God created." In reply, a Manichaean teacher named Faustus argued that because this passage contradicts the message that Paul preached to Thecla, Paul could not have written it.[49] The legends fought back! Perhaps there is no better way to end our discussion of the battle for Paul's memory than merely to transcribe excerpts from Faustus' straightforward, revealing, and remarkable arguments against the Pastoral Epistles:

> Consider, I beseech you, if it is not perfect madness to suppose these words to be Paul's, that abstinence from food and forbidding to marry are doctrines of devils. Paul cannot have said that to dedicate virgins to Christ is a doctrine of devils. But you read the words, and inconsiderately, as usual, apply them to us, without seeing that *this stamps your virgins too*

as led away by the doctrine of devils, and that you are the functionaries of the devils in your constant endeavors to induce virgins to make this profession, *so that in all your churches the virgins nearly out-number the married women.* Why do you still adhere to such practises? . . . If you say that to encourage the proposal . . . is all the doctrine of devils, . . . *the apostle himself will be thus brought into danger, if he must be considered as having introduced the doctrines of devils into Iconium, when Thecla, after having been betrothed, was by his discourse inflamed with the desire of perpetual virginity. . . .* I do not mention other apostles of our Lord, Peter, Andrew, Thomas, and the example of celibacy, the blessed John, who in various ways commended to young men and maidens the excellence of this profession, leaving to us, and to you too, the form for making virgins. I do not mention them, because you do not admit them into the canon, and so you will not scruple impiously to impute to them the doctrines of devils. *But will you say the same of Christ, or of the Apostle Paul, who, we know, everywhere expressed the same preference for unmarried women to the married, and gave an example of it in the case of the saintly Thecla? But if the doctrine preached by Paul to Thecla, and which* the other apostles also preached, was not the doctrine of devils, how can *we believe that Paul left on record his opinion, that the very exhortation to sanctity is the injunction and the doctrine of devils?*[50]

No less remarkable is Augustine's response. He does not deny Paul's preference for celibacy, nor the reliability of the Thecla tradition, nor the claim that Catholic virgins nearly outnumbered married women. He simply argued that whereas Catholics teach that "marriage is good, and virginity better,"[51] Manichaeans made marriage a heinous sin. They made allowances for sexual intercourse, but discouraged marriage, and considered procreation the enslaving of divine particles in the material world. As Augustine put it, Manichaeans "would have thought better of Mary had she ceased to be a virgin without being a mother, than as being a mother without ceasing to be a virgin."[52] But Faustus saw more clearly than Augustine that the statements concerning sexuality in the Pastoral Epistles were inconsistent not only with Manichaean practice but also with the Catholic predilection for virginity and the veneration of Thecla. In the ancient battle for Paul's memory there were no decisive victors. Both the Pastoral Epistles and the legends won—and lost.[53]

CONCLUSION

Even though in antiquity both the Pastoral Epistles and the legend tradition scored victories, in the centuries between Augustine and the present time the Pastorals have become the sole victors. As the Bible gained importance as a source of authority for the church the legend tradition inevitably lost ground. When the Protestant Reformers insisted on *sola scriptura* they effectively removed the Paul of legendary memory from serious theological consideration and then deported him to the remotest corners of the church's self-consciousness, to regions traveled only by historians who enjoy collecting early Christian esoterica. Consequently, the modern church has amnesia of this aspect of its past.

In this book I have tried to bring the legendary memory of Paul back from its exile in near oblivion and to place it properly within the second-century development of Pauline tradition. Doing this has shown that the Pastorals did not develop linearly from Paul's ministry but dialectically; that is, they were written to oppose another strand of Pauline tradition whose legends depicted him as a social radical. There was indeed a battle for Paul's memory.

Many factors drove the wedge between these two traditions: gender, social status, literacy, and doubtless many others. But the most important single source of the polarization was the complexity of Paul himself.[1] If any one true statement could be made concerning interpretations of Paul from antiquity to the present, it would be this: Paul has become "all things to all people." Wayne Meeks, an eminent New Testament scholar, after describing how radically modern interpretations of Paul differ from one another, concluded that Paul is a "Christian Proteus," like the Proteus of the *Odyssey*, a sea daemon who eluded capture by continually changing his form.[2] So too in the ancient church the author of the Pastoral Epistles grasped Paul in one of his shapes; the storytellers grasped another; but neither captured him. Neither compares with Menelaus, who finally learned Proteus' secrets because he persistently held on to the daemon until he had transformed himself into a lion, a serpent, a leopard, a boar, water, and a tree. Likewise, to understand Paul is to see him in his many masks, to wrestle with him in his many forms. Herein lies the ultimate victory of the legends: they remind us that the interpretation of Paul in the Pastoral Epistles was not the only one permissible within the Pauline heritage.

In fact, in many respects the legends stand closer to the center of Paul's theology than do the Pastorals. Paul believed that because the present is the age of the Spirit—discontinuous with the age of the law and anticipatory of the age to come—the Christian community already experiences the joy, freedom, and unity of the kingdom of God. It had broken with the past and its various forms of bondage. Consequently, he thought of baptism as an initiation into that community of the future where distinctions between races, social classes, and sexes no longer applied:

> For as many of you as were baptized into Christ have put on
> Christ. There is neither Jew nor Greek, there is neither slave
> nor free, there is neither male nor female; for you are all one
> in Christ Jesus. (Gal. 3:27–28)

In other words, by depicting Paul as an apocalyptic sectarian who preached manumission and sexual equality the legends transmitted bits of the Pauline memory with undeniable claims on the historical Paul.

There can be little doubt that women exercised important leadership in Pauline circles. Romans 16 alone mentions ten women as workers with him; one is called a deacon, another an apostle (vs. 1 and 7). In 1 Cor. 11:2–16, Paul opposes women who removed their veils while praying and prophesying, but he never objects to their speaking in the congregation. Slaves too fared better in the Pauline communities than the author of the Pastorals would have us believe. Because the slave Onesimus had become a Christian, Paul sends him back to his master with a letter requesting Philemon either to manumit him or to send him, as his slave, to attend to Paul's needs as he travels.[3] Had Paul lived into the second century, he surely would have resented reading in the Pastoral Epistles that he allegedly had silenced women and barred slaves from freedom.

He also would have been surprised to read that he had tried to preserve the faith by handing on his teachings to Timothy and Titus and from them to later bishops. To be sure, Paul valued his own ministry and trusted these two men—among others—with extending his influence. But he also recognized that neither he nor they had a monopoly on the gospel.[4] Furthermore, Paul may not have recognized a bishop if he saw one. The word *episkopos* appears only in Phil. 1:1 in all of Paul's letters, and here it may retain its original, generic meaning as "one who oversees" and not its later, technical meaning as "bishop." Philippians 1:1 may not even be authentically Pauline. Because Philippians almost certainly is a collection of three Pauline fragments assembled at a later date,[5] the first two verses might very well be the work of assemblers, perhaps generated from other Pauline openings (cf. 2 Cor. 1:1–2; 1 Thess. 1:1; 2 Thess. 1:1–2; Philemon 1–3). Be that as it may, Paul's understanding of leadership in the church is democratic, not hierarchical. He likens the church to a body in which all parts have their importance (e.g., 1 Cor. 12:12–31), and not to a royal dynasty, as in the Pastorals.

Paul and the author of the Pastorals also disagree concerning celibacy. Although Paul does not forbid marriage, as the legend tradition would have us think, he does discourage it. Both men and women should remain celibate in order to devote themselves more intensely to "the affairs of the Lord," providing they can bridle their sexual desires (1 Cor. 7:25–38). The author of the Pastorals, who undoubtedly knew 1 Corinthians and its appeals for celibacy,[6] intentionally reversed the apostle's preference by requiring all church leaders to marry.

What, then, shall we do with the Pastorals? Shall we dismiss them as nothing more than brilliant forgeries documenting the decadence of Paulinism in the second century? No! On the contrary, it is only when we read the Pastorals against the backdrop of the legend tradition that we can see behind them a development of Pauline tradition with its own integrity and its own contributions to Christian theology.

There can be no doubt that the Pastoral Epistles are children of the Pauline mission and heirs of his legacy. For their author, as for Paul, grace is the gift of life in Christ (1 Tim. 1:14), and love the goal (1:5). In spite of his accommodation to the standards of Asia Minor society, the author retained Paul's conviction that Christian existence is participation in the sufferings of Christ: "All who desire to live a godly life in Christ Jesus will be persecuted" (2 Tim. 3:12). "The saying is sure: If we have died with him, we shall also live with him; if we endure, we shall also reign with him" (2:11–12a). Even though the Pastorals are not apocalyptic, they share Paul's hope in the return of Christ (1 Tim. 6:14–16; 2 Tim. 1:12; 4:8; Titus 2:13–14). The following excerpt masterfully weaves these themes together into a fabric worthy of Paul himself.

> Do not be ashamed then of testifying to our Lord, nor of me
> his prisoner, but share in suffering for the gospel in the
> power of God, who saved us and called us with a holy calling,

> not in virtue of our works but in virtue of his own purpose
> and the grace which he gave us in Christ Jesus ages ago, and
> now has manifested through the appearing of our Savior
> Christ Jesus, who abolished death and brought life and
> immortality to light through the gospel. (2 Tim. 1:8–10)

Furthermore, the repeated concern in the Pastorals that Christians not give unnecessary offense to outsiders is itself a development of Paul's ideas. For example, in 1 Cor. 10:32–33 we read: "Give no offense to Jews or to Greeks or to the church of God, just as I try to please all people in everything I do"; and in 1 Thess. 4:10b–12a: "But we exhort you . . . to aspire to live quietly, to mind your own affairs, and to work with your hands, . . . so that you may command the respect of outsiders."

But in the Pastorals this sensitivity to the perceptions of outsiders is reshaped by the author's awareness of the dangers of sectarianism. Because sectarian communities define themselves over against dominant cultures and thus emphasize their ethical distinctiveness, they sometimes fail to appreciate fully their affirmation of God as the creator of the world. For example, even though the *Acts of Paul* argues against Gnostics, who attributed the creation to a lesser, fallen power, it never expresses a natural theology extolling the goodness of the world or inspiring love and responsibility for it. When the *Acts of Paul* affirms God's creation of the world, it does so primarily to show that God also has the power to destroy it. Believers are not to embrace the world, but are to flee it. "Blessed are they who have renounced this world, for they shall be well pleasing unto God. . . . Blessed are they who through love of God have departed from the form of this world, for they shall judge angels" (3:5 and 6). According to the legends, the flesh is wanton; sex is sin; wine, meat, money, and fine clothes are shackles to the soul.

The Pastorals, however, recognize that absolute celibacy and proscriptions of foods devalue the world that God made "to be received with thanksgiving by those who believe and know the truth. For everything created by God is good, and nothing is to be rejected if it is received with thanksgiving" (1 Tim. 4:3b–4; cf. Titus 1:15–16). In this respect the author again develops a Pauline insight: "For 'the earth is the Lord's, and everything in it.' If one of the unbelievers invites you to dinner and you are disposed to go, eat whatever is set before you without raising any question on the ground of conscience" (1 Cor. 10:26–27). Or again: "I know and am persuaded in the Lord Jesus that nothing is unclean in itself; but it is unclean for any one who thinks it unclean" (Rom 14:14).

Furthermore the Pastorals expand the rule of God from the sect to the world, thereby suggesting to the church that God is at work in society at large, that outsiders too can experience God, be devout, and live morally. We have seen this exclusiveness repeatedly in the *Acts of Paul*. But the author of the Pastorals reminds his readers that "the grace of God has appeared for the salvation of *all* people" (Titus 2:11). God "is the savior of *all* people, especially of those who believe" (1 Tim. 4:10). Here it would appear that the author thinks salvation is available outside the church. Furthermore, he insists that Christians pray not just for themselves but for *all* people, inasmuch as by so doing they will "lead a quiet and peaceable life" (1 Tim. 2:1–2). Similarly, he tells his readers than even though Roman society did not share all the values of the church, Roman morality did not always conflict with the church. Instead of competing with the moral expectations of society, the church heightened them. The most important contribution of the Pastorals to Christian theology may be their reminder that Christ can be seen not only in the Christian community but also in nature and culture. In antiquity this insight was transmitted through various kinds of *logos* Christologies (i.e., Christ is the principle or reason behind the order of the universe, including human society), and has been reaffirmed powerfully in the twentieth century in some process theologies.

Therefore, it is clear that the Pastoral Epistles deserve a hearing from us, but our decision as to *how* we shall hear them carries with it momentous results for the church. Some insist that the Pastorals and the authentic Pauline letters came from the same hand. They do so either by minimizing the differences between them, or by appealing to exceptional conditions in the production of the Pastorals. For example, some would claim that Paul wrote the Pastorals with the help of an amanuensis, or secretary, to whom he gave considerable liberty in composition, or that he wrote differently to individuals than he did to churches, or that he wrote the Pastorals later in life when he had changed his mind on certain matters. The tragedy of such theories is not only that they fail to distinguish between Paul and his pseudonymous interpreter, but worse, they allow the reactionism of the Pastorals to take even firmer root in the church. Fortunately, because these theories overlook other insurmountable obstacles to the Pauline authorship of the Pastorals they have few scholarly defenders today.

Most scholars agree that someone other than Paul wrote the Pastoral Epistles, but many of them nonetheless suppose that the author stood in the mainstream of later Pauline tradition. According to them, the author sought to redefine the Pauline message in order to render it more palatable, and to defend it against heresy. Some even speak of the author's domestication of Paul as legitimate, healthy, and inevitable.

This interpretation fails to see that any judgment we make about the mainstream of Pauline tradition comes not from understanding the circumstances that produced the Pastorals but from prejudices derived from later developments in the church. As we have seen, the tradition splintered off in several directions, each claiming to be the mainstream.

Once we recognize that the Pastorals represent but one option within Pauline tradition, we are obligated to decide which of the interpretations of Paul we shall prefer. It is not sufficient simply to appeal to the New Testament canon, for even though the canonizing of the New Testament in some respects served the interests of Christians more conciliatory to the dominant society, the New Testament nonetheless retains much of the apocalyptic sectarianism of the early church. The authentic letters of Paul, the Gospel of Mark, and the Revelation of John all pulled against the wave of cultural accommodation that swept along the Pastorals and crested in the fourth century with the christianizing of the empire under Constantine and Theodosius. This tugging of the New Testament books against themselves generates power which none of them could have had individually. It sets us interpreters aswirl among the competing theological currents, and forces us to choose which of them we shall let direct us. Some of the strongest currents flowing against the Pastorals come from the authentic letters of Paul.

Therefore, although the New Testament does not contain the *Acts of Paul,* it does contain two competing images of Paul to which we must respond: the Paul of the genuine epistles and the Paul of the Pastorals. The decision of the church to canonize both shows that neither can be ignored, but precisely because these images compete with each other one must choose which one will be more normative. I choose the Paul of the genuine epistles. I do so not just as a historian in quest of the historical Paul, nor just as a humanist who opposes slavery, sexism, and other institutions of inhumanity. I do so also as a Christian committed to the church. The annals of the church chronicle the tragic results of its conformity to dehumanizing social conventions and its complicity with political power. In every age the church has faced the same dilemma: Will it serve Christ or Caesar? Will it be a prophet faithful to its tradition and values regardless of their unpopularity, or will it merely be a priest writing sacred footnotes for the dominant cultural script? Only when it embodies the rule of God and wrestles against its environment can the church claim its central symbol: the cross of Jesus.

Herein lies the ultimate victory of the women who told these ancient legends: by revealing how churches in the Pauline circle struggled against their environments, they prevent us from assuming that the domestication of the gospel in the Pastoral Epistles was an inevitable development of the Pauline mission. Paul's charge that Christians not be conformed to the world continued to be a part of the Pauline legacy— and still is. The battle for Paul's memory continues to be waged whenever we feel the tension between our affirmation that God created the world and our calling to transform it.

NOTES

INTRODUCTION

1. Apuleius, *The Golden Ass* 4, 28. The translation is adapted from that of Robert Graves, *The Golden Ass of Apuleius*, p. 86.

2. Apuleius, *The Golden Ass* 6, 25 (translation from Graves, p. 130).

3. Plato, *Republic* II, 377C. The translation comes from G. M. A. Grube in *Plato's Republic*, p. 47.

4. See also Dio Chrysostom, *Discourses* 4, 73–74; Philostratus the Elder, *Imagines* 1, 15; Flavius Philostratus, *Life of Apollonius of Tyana* 5, 14; Cicero, *On the Nature of the Gods* 1, 34, and 3, 5; Horace, *Satires* 2, 6, 77; Quintilian, *Institutes* 1, 8, 19, and 1, 9, 2; and among Christian authors Minucius Felix, *Octavius* 20, and Lactantius, *Divine Institutes* 3, 18. Ovid, *Metamorphoses* 4, 31 begins a series of tales told by women.

5. The legacy of Paul in the second century has received much scholarly attention and remains a fertile area of research. Among the more important studies are those by Eva Aleith, *Paulusverständnis in der alten Kirche*, BZNW 18; Albert E. Barnett, *Paul Becomes a Literary Influence*; Ernst Dassmann, *Der Stachel im Fleisch. Paulus in der frühchristlichen Literatur bis Irenäus;* Hans von Campenhausen, *The Formation of the Christian Bible*, trans. by J. A. Baker; Elaine Hiesey Pagels, *The Gnostic Paul: Gnostic Exegesis of the Pauline Letters;* and especially Andreas Lindemann, *Paulus im ältesten Christentum. Das Bild des Apostels und die Rezeption der paulinischen Theologie in der frühchristlichen Literatur bis Marcion*, BHT 58, and David K. Rensberger, "As the Apostle Teaches: The Development of the Use of Paul's Letters in Second-Century Christianity," Ph.D. dissertation. Unlike the foregoing studies, the present book restricts its purview to those developments of the Pauline tradition pertinent to Asia Minor, and gives far more attention to the legendary memory of the apostle.

CHAPTER I. The Oral Legends Behind the *Acts of Paul*

1. "But if they claim writings which are wrongly inscribed with Paul's name—I mean the example of Thecla—in support of women's freedom to teach and baptize, let them know that a presbyter in Asia, who put together that book, heaping up a narrative as it were from his own materials under Paul's name, when after conviction he confessed that he had done it from love of Paul,

resigned his position" (Tertullian, *On Baptism* I, 17, as quoted in *A New Eusebius: Documents Illustrative of the History of the Church to A.D. 337*, ed. by James Stevenson, p. 184. For a discussion of the textual variant on this passage that explicitly refers to the *Acts of Paul*, see A. Souter, "The 'Acta Pauli' etc. in Tertullian," *JTS* 25 (1924): 292.

2. Origen, *Commentary on the Gospel of St. John* 20, 12, and *On First Principles* 1, 2, 3.

3. Eusebius, *Ecclesiastical History* 3, 3, 5 and 3, 25, 4; and Jerome, *On Illustrious Men* 7.

4. The *Acts of Paul* was used by Manichaeans and Priscillians.

5. Carl Schmidt, *Acta Pauli aus der Heidelberger koptischen Papyrushandschrift Nr. 1*, and with Wilhelm Schubart, *Praxeis Paulou: Acta Pauli nach dem Papyrus der Hamburger Staats- und Universitäts-Bibliothek*.

6. For a judicious discussion of the origin of the *Acts of Paul*, see Léon Vouaux in *Les Actes de Paul et ses lettres apocryphes: introduction, textes, traduction et commentaire*, 97–112.

7. Adolf von Harnack: "The hypothesis is completely adequate that the author did not freely invent everything, but rather relies upon an oral tradition which dragged on throughout a century and also preserved a few small characteristic touches. How far the actual events extend, how far the legendary traditions which the author lit upon, how far finally his own additions—to determine this all means are lacking" (*Geschichte der altchristlichen Literatur bis Eusebius*, Part 2, *Die Chronologie*, 2d ed., 1. 505, as quoted in *New Testament Apocrypha*, ed. by Edgar Hennecke and Wilhelm Schneemelcher, 2.333). Fortunately, Harnack's pessimism about detecting the stages of composition must now be qualified because of the enormous methodological advances in this century.

8. For pioneering studies in the area of folk stories and early Christianity, see Paul Wendland, *De fabellis antiquis earumque ad Christianos propagatione*, and *Die urchristlichen Literaturformen*, HNT 1, 3; Richard Reitzenstein, *Hellenistische Wundererzählungen*, 3d ed.; Hippolyte Delehaye, *Die hagiographischen Legenden*, trans. by E. A. Stückelberg; and A. J. Festugière, "Lieux Communs littéraires et thèmes de folk-lore dans l'hagiographie primitive," *Wiener Studien* 73 (1960).

9. Some folklorists doom to failure all studies of orality in written texts. For example, see Francis Lee Utley, "Folk Literature: An Operational Definition," in *The Study of Folklore*, ed. by Alan Dundes, pp. 18–19.

10. Hennecke and Schneemelcher (eds.), *New Testament Apocrypha* 2.

11. See Ilana Dan, "The Innocent Persecuted Heroine: An Attempt at a Model for the Surface Level of the Narrative Structure of the Female Fairy Tale," in *Patterns in Oral Literature*, ed. by Heda Jason and Dimitri Segal, pp. 13–30. It might prove profitable to compare the Thecla story with the pattern detected by Dan in AT (Aarne-Thompson) story types 403 (The black and the white bride), 706 (The maiden without hands), 712 (Crescentia), and 883 A (The innocent slandered maiden). I have already done so superficially, and have discovered many suggestive similarities. However, I have not yet been able to harmonize Dan's analysis of the functions of *dramatis personae* with my own analysis of the discourse texture. Furthermore, because the Thecla story is not a romance like those studied by Dan, it is likely that one would find alterations in the structure as well. Regardless, AT 403, 706, and 883A afford clear proof of the popularity in oral tradition of the themes of the Thecla story.

12. Ludwig Radermacher, *Hippolytus und Thekla. Studien zur Geschichte von Legende und Kultus,* Kaiserliche Akademie der Wissenschaften in Wien. Philosophisch-historische Klasse. Sitzungsberichte 182, 3.

13. Ibid., pp. 70–79.

14. Ibid., pp. 83–92. Having recognized similarities between the apocryphal Acts of apostles and Hellenistic romances, some scholars have gone so far as to categorize the Acts as Christian romances. See, for example, Rosa Söder, *Die apokryphen Apostelgeschichten und die romanhafte Literatur der Antike,* Würzburger Studien zur Altertumswissenschaft 3. For a critical treatment of Söder, see Jean-Daniel Kaestli, "Les Principales Orientations de la recherche sur les Actes apocryphes," in *Les Actes apocryphes des Apôtres,* ed. by François Bovon, Publications de la faculté de théologie de l'Université de Genève 4, pp. 49–67, especially pp. 57–67. Radermacher's analysis of the Hippolytus/Thecla tale type would suggest that the similarities between the romances and the apocryphal Acts are due in part to their common debts to popular oral legends. To my knowledge, no scholar has attempted to develop this line of research, even though both genres are dependent on oral traditions. For example, in Apuleius' *The Golden Ass* an old woman tells a younger woman the story of Cupid and Psyche, and in Longus' *Daphnis and Chloe* we find two folk tales: the legend of Echo, and a story about a girl who became a bird.

15. Mary Grant, *The Myths of Hyginus,* p. 1.

16. Ibid., p. 176.

17. See Richard Adelbert Lipsius and Maximilian Bonnet (eds.), *Acta apostolorum apocrypha* 1.269–272.

18. William Mitchell Ramsay, "The Acta of Paul and Thekla," in *The Church in the Roman Empire Before A.D. 170,* pp. 382–389.

19. David Magie, *Roman Rule in Asia Minor to the End of the Third Century After Christ,* 1.513, and 2.1368.

20. The arguments for an Ephesian destination of Romans 16 are as follows: (1) letters of recommendation were common in Pauline circles (e.g., Acts 18:27; 2 Cor. 3:1–3; 8:16–23), (2) vs. 30–33 of Romans 15, which include a benediction and a final Amen, appear to be the end of a letter, (3) the admonition in 16:17–20 that the recipients avoid those who were creating dissentions seems to be unrelated to anything in the rest of Romans, and it has an authoritarian spirit unlike that in the rest of the book, (4) Paul probably would not have addressed so many people with intimate greetings in a letter to a church he had never visited, (5) Aquila and Priscilla, mentioned in vs. 3–4, were last mentioned in connection with Ephesus (1 Cor. 16:19; cf. Acts 18:24–28), and (6) in v. 5 Epaenetus is called the first convert in Asia.

21. For a discussion of the evidence for a historical Thecla, see Henri Leclercq, *Les Martyrs,* 1.155–163.

22. Vouaux, *Actes,* 24–69.

23. Jerome's rejection of the *Acts of Paul* appears in *On Illustrious Men* 7, and his praise of Thecla in his *Letter to Eustochium.*

24. Cesare Baronius, *Martyrologium romanum* (Venice, 1593), p. 434.

25. For example, "After she had been freed from judgment, she pursued the chase for Paul, and guided by heavenly voices she took courage on the roads that led to Paul. The Devil, however, was watching the maiden, and when he had watched her travel down the road, he marched in the suitor against the girl, like a thief of virginity in the desert. And as the noble woman continued on her way,

the suitor, with the lewdness of a horse, lying in wait behind her, shouted for joy at the thought of seizing her. There was no exit anywhere. The attacker was strong, and the one attacked was frail. Where was there any refuge in a desert for shelter?" When Thecla cried out to God, "she became invisible and the suitor went away having gained only one thing: a horse race of licentiousness." (Translation mine)

26. See Lipsius and Bonnet (eds.), *Acta apostolorum apocrypha* 1.269–272.

27. See A. J. Festugière, *Sainte Thècle, saints Côme et Damien, saints Cyr et Jean (extraits), saint Georges,* Collections grecques des miracles, 11–20.

28. See also the articles on Thecla in *DACL* 15.2225–2235, and in *Bibliotheca Hagiographica Graeca,* 3d ed., 2.267–269.

29. Robert E. Osborne, "Paul and the Wild Beasts," *JBL* 85 (1966):228. The inscription reads: *ho leo[n]to anagnous leichei sōt/ēr[a t]on hypo tauron.*

30. Hippolytus, *Commentary on Daniel* 3.29 (GCS 1.176); translation mine.

31. For example, Vouaux, *Actes,* 24–27.

32. *Canon Muratori* does not mention the *Acts of Paul.* Vouaux has carefully collected patristic allusions to the *Acts of Paul,* and none of them come from the West, except for Hippolytus' allusion to Paul and the lion (*Actes,* 24–69).

33. Ignatius, *Romans* 5:2 (Loeb).

34. Dennis Ronald MacDonald, "A Conjectural Emendation of 1 Cor. 15:31–32: Or the Case of the Misplaced Lion Fight," *HTR* 73 (1980):265–276.

35. Acts 20:23; 21:11–14; 28:30; Clement of Rome, *1 Clement* 5:5–7; Ignatius, *Ephesians* 12:12.

36. Eusebius, *Ecclesiastical History* 3, 39, 9.

37. Ignatius does not list poison among means of execution used against Christians (*Romans* 5:3 and *Smyrneans* 4:2), nor is there a single reference to death by poison in Herbert Musurillo's *Acts of the Christian Martyrs: Introduction, Texts and Translations.* Some editions of the *Acts of John* contain a trial by ordeal using poison, but this story probably was added to the book much later (Hennecke and Schneemelcher, eds., *New Testament Apocrypha* 2.204–206).

38. See Vouaux, *Actes,* 113–124.

39. Hennecke and Schneemelcher (eds.), *New Testament Apocrypha* 2.348.

40. Alex Olrik, "Epic Laws of Folk Narrative," in *The Study of Folklore,* ed. by Alan Dundes, pp. 131–141.

41. Ibid., p. 130.

42. See Heda Jason and Dimitri Segal, "Introduction," in *Patterns in Oral Literature,* ed. by Heda Jason and Dimitri Segal, pp. 1–10.

43. Olrik, "Epic Laws," pp. 131–132.

44. Ibid., p. 139.

45. Ibid.

46. Ibid., p. 135.

47. Ibid.

48. Ibid., p. 136.

49. *AP* 11:7.

50. Olrik, "Epic Laws," p. 137.

51. Vladímir Propp, the great Russian folklorist, called such back-referencing "notification," and showed that it could take two forms: (1) references to the past for the benefit of the hearer/reader, and (2) those for the benefit of the other characters within the story (*Morphology of the Folktale,* trans. by Laurence Scott

with an introduction by Svatava Pirkova-Jakobson; 2d ed. rev. and ed. with a preface by Louis A. Wagner, and with a new introduction by Alan Dundes, pp. 71–74). The back reference to the baptized lion was of the first type, but the second also appears in our stories. When new characters enter the narrative whom the storyteller wishes to inform about the past in order to make them as omniscient as the hearer/reader, instead of repeating the story in detail, the storyteller simply says "and X told Y all that had happened" and the hearer/reader fills in the background information immediately. This convention appears over and over again in our stories. This abbreviated form of notification is also used as shorthand for giving the content of Paul's proclamation. Paul's first speech is quite long and contains all the basic elements of his message necessary for understanding his fate in the story (3:5–6). Thereafter, however, when Paul preaches to new characters the storyteller needs only to say "Paul taught them the Word of God" (e.g., 3:39 and 40).

52. Olrik, "Epic Laws," pp. 132–133.

53. Ibid., p. 138.

54. "She appears sometimes with the head of a lion or writhing serpents at her feet, surrounded by various instruments of torture, bound to a stake, the flames shrinking away from her, or tied to two bulls, the cords which gird her being about to break ... and seated or kneeling in the amphitheatre with the wild beasts about her" (Nancy R. E. Bell, *Lives and Legends of the Evangelists, Apostles, and Other Early Saints*, p. 189).

55. Olrik, "Epic Laws," p. 132.

56. Vouaux gives a French translation of the text in *Actes*, 25–26.

57. Albert B. Lord, *The Singer of Tales* p. 94.

CHAPTER II. The Storytellers Behind the Legends

1. Stevan L. Davies, *The Revolt of the Widows: The Social World of the Apocryphal Acts*, pp. 105–109. During a session at the 1981 Annual Meeting of the Society of Biblical Literature, Davies argued that Tertullian did not fabricate the entire episode but spoke of some other document now lost. The claim by Margaret Howe that Thecla represents women in restricted roles completely misses the point ("Interpretations of Paul in the Acts of Paul and Thecla," in *Pauline Studies*, ed. by Donald A. Hagner and Murray J. Harris, pp. 33–49).

2. Eusebius, *Ecclesiastical History* 5, 17, 4, and Origen's fragment on 1 Corinthians, no. 74, published by Claude Jenkins, "Origen on 1 Corinthians," *JTS* 10 (1908–09):41–42.

3. Epiphanius, *Panarion* 49, 2. All we know of the Quintillians is what we learn from Epiphanius. It would appear that they were a fourth-century offshoot of Montanism in Asia Minor.

4. Eusebius, *Ecclesiastical History* 3, 39, 9.

5. Tertullian, *Prescription Against Heretics* 30; Hippolytus, *Refutation of All Heresies* 7, 26; and Theodoret, *Compendium of Heretical Fables* 1, 25.

6. Eusebius, *Ecclesiastical History* 5, 16, 17.

7. Theodoret, *Compendium of Heretical Fables* 3, 2; Didymus, *On the Trinity* 3, 41, 3.

8. The précis is of *AP* 3:26–39.

9. Davies, *The Revolt of the Widows*, p. 107.

10. See pp. 24–25.

11. Philip of Side, *Church History* (TU 5, 2.170); cf. Eusebius, *Ecclesiastical History* 3, 39, 9. The name Manaemus may be a corruption of Manaen, who appears in Acts 13:1 as one of Paul's companions.

12. Eusebius, *Ecclesiastical History* 3, 39, 17.

13. According to Ramsay, "The Acta of Paul and Thekla," in his *The Church in the Roman Empire Before A.D. 170*, pp. 390–410.

14. For the arguments supporting the Ephesian destination of Romans 16, see p. 107 n. 20.

15. 1 Cor. 16:19; cf. Acts 18:2, 18, 26.

16. Philemon 1–2.

17. Col. 4:15. Phoebe of Cenchreae and Chloe of Corinth also may have entertained house churches (Rom. 16:1–2; 1 Cor. 1:11).

18. Raymond E. Brown, *The Community of the Beloved Disciple*, pp. 183–198.

19. Proclus according to Eusebius, *Ecclesiastical History* 3, 31, 4 (cf. 2, 25, 6). But Polycrates, the bishop of Ephesus, wrote Victor of Rome that the virgin daughters of Philip who lived in Hierapolis were sired by Philip the apostle, not the evangelist (*Ecclesiastical History* 3, 31, 3, and 5, 24, 2). Furthermore, Clement of Alexandria says that Philip—the evangelist or the apostle?—gave his daughters in marriage (*Stromateis* 3, 6, 52). In attempting to harmonize these references some scholars have suggested that both Philips had daughters. The apostle and his daughters moved to Hierapolis, while the evangelist and his daughters presumably stayed in Caesarea, and perhaps were given in marriage as Clement says (H. J. Lawlor and J. E. L. Oulton, *Eusebius: The Ecclesiastical History and the Martyrs of Palestine*, 2.116–118). But this theory assumes that both Philips had at least three daughters who were renowned virgins. I prefer the explanation of the evidence offered by Peter Corssen, who identifies the women in Acts 21 with those in Hierapolis ("Die Töchter des Philippus," *ZNW* 2 [1901]:238–299).

20. Quoted by Apollinarius of Hierapolis in Eusebius, *Ecclesiastical History* 5, 17, 2–4.

21. Compare Ignatius, *Smyrneans* 13:2, and the *Martyrdom of Polycarp* 17:2. Ignatius also sent greetings to "the house of Tavia (or Gabia)" in Smyrna, which may indicate that the community met in her home (*Smyrneans* 13:2).

22. Pliny, *Letters* 10, 96, 8.

23. Nunes, Strateges, Pribu, and Matrona in eastern Phrygia (at Axylos); Masa, Aurelia Faustina, Paula, and Timothea in Cilicia (at Laodicea Combusta and Korykos); Arete in Caria (at Aphrodisias); and Elaphia in Nevinne. See Roger Gryson, *The Ministry of Women in the Early Church*, trans. by Jean Laporte and Mary Louise Hall, pp. 90–91.

24. *Martyrdom of Carpus, Papylus, and Agathonice* 42–47.

25. Epiphanius, *Panarion* 49, 2, quoting Gal. 3:28.

26. Cyprian, *Epistles* 74, 10 and 11.

27. Irenaeus, *Against Heresies* 1, 13, 2–3.

28. Epiphanius, *Panarion* 26, 1, 3; cf. Philaster of Brescia, *Book of the Heresies* 33, 3. Nicolaitans are mentioned in Rev. 2:6 and 15.

29. *The Hypostasis of the Archons* and *The Thought of Norea*.

30. *On the Origin of the World*, CG II, 102, 10–11, and 24–25.

31. Of course, Gnostics frequently venerated women revealers, and not only in Asia Minor; e.g., see Origen, *Against Celsus* 5, 62.

32. Hippolytus, *Refutation of All Heresies* 5, 7, 1.

33. According to Douglas M. Parrott in *The Nag Hammadi Library in English*, ed. by James M. Robinson, p. 207.

34. Eusebius, *Ecclesiastical History* 3, 31, 3.

35. Ibid., 3, 18, 3.

36. Epiphanius, *Panarion* 49, 2.

37. Marcion, Julius Cassianus, the *Gospel of the Egyptians* (in Clement of Alexandria), the *Gospel of Thomas*, the *Acts of Thomas*, and the *Gospel of Philip*, to name a few.

38. Ignatius, *Smyrneans* 13:1.

39. "In a certain place a virgin of less than twenty years of age has been placed in the order of widows" (Tertullian, *On the Veiling of Virgins* 9, ANF). This "certain place" undoubtedly was in Asia Minor. Before writing this Latin treatise Tertullian had already gone to the trouble of writing one in Greek, which certainly suggests the objectionable practice of not veiling virgins obtained in the Greek East. But Greece was not the place, for he says explicitly that all adult Greek women wore veils—even in Corinth (8). Furthermore, the congregations where virgins were not veiled were founded by "apostles and apostolic people" (2). Tertullian called this virgin-widow a monstrosity. This attitude, so unlike Ignatius', probably reflects the different way African churches supported single women. African (and Syrian) churches had a separate order of virgins, but there was no such distinction in Asia Minor. Needy women who had taken the pledge to celibacy were simply enrolled with the widows and shared their title.

40. See William R. Bascom, "Folklore and Anthropology," in *The Study of Folklore*, ed. by Dundes, p. 26.

41. See Madonna Kolbenschlag, *Kiss Sleeping Beauty Good-Bye: Breaking the Spell of Feminine Myths and Models*.

42. William Hugh Jansen, "The Esoteric-Exoteric Factor in Folklore," in *The Study of Folklore*, ed. by Dundes, pp. 43–51.

43. For a discussion of the responsibilities of the Galatarch and the Asiarch, see Magie, *Roman Rule in Asia Minor to the End of the Third Century After Christ*, 2.1298–1301 and 1318–1319.

44. Ibid., 836–839. See also F. C. Conybeare, *The Armenian Apology and Acts of Apollonius*, 2d ed. The special note on p. 80 refers to a bust in the Vatican Museum (n. 280) bearing just such a wreath.

45. Magie lists a Titus Claudius Alexander as a Galatarch (*Roman Rule* 2.1609).

46. Conybeare, *Armenian Apology*, pp. 76–77.

47. These verses trade on the Nero redivivus myth. See Suetonius, *Life of Nero* 57; Tacitus, *Histories* 2, 8 and 9; and Dio Cassius, *Roman History* 64, 9.

48. Tertullian's treatise *The Chaplet* was prompted by the refusal of a Christian soldier to wear a wreath in honor of the emperor. Tertullian justifies the action because the wreath was identified with idolatry, but he does not tell us whether the wreath bore imperial insignia.

49. 1 John 3:13; Ignatius, *Romans* 3:3; cf. John 15:18–19.

50. Pliny, *Letters* 10, 96.

51. Eusebius, *Ecclesiastical History* 4, 8, 6—9, 3 (cf. 4, 12, 1—13, 8).

52. Ibid., 4, 3, 1.

53. Ibid., 4, 26, 5–6.

54. Ibid., 4, 26, 6.

55. E.g., Athenagoras, *A Plea Regarding Christians* 3, 31 and 35; Justin, *First*

Apology 26, 7; Tatian, *Oration to the Greeks* 25, 3; and Tertullian, *Apology* 7, 1.

56. Tertullian, *To Scapula* 5 (ANF).

57. For an excellent treatment of the roots of hostility in Asia Minor between church and society, see John H. Elliot, *A Home for the Homeless: A Sociological Exegesis of 1 Peter, Its Situation and Strategy*, pp. 21–100.

58. Victor Turner, *The Ritual Process: Structure and Anti-Structure*, pp. 111–112. Examples of such groups may be found in Norman Cohn, *The Pursuit of the Millennium: Revolutionary Millenarians and Mystical Anarchists of the Middle Ages*, rev. ed. See also John G. Gager, *Kingdom and Community: The Social World of Early Christianity*, and Gerd Theissen, *Sociology of Early Palestinian Christianity*, trans. by John Bowden.

59. "Woman, ruler of this world, mistress of much gold, citizen of great luxury, splendid in thy raiment, sit down on the floor and forget thy riches and thy beauty and thy finery. For these will profit thee nothing if thou pray not to God who regards as dross all that here is imposing, but graciously bestows what there is wonderful. Gold perishes, riches are consumed, clothes become worn out. Beauty grows old, and great cities are changed, and the world will be destroyed in fire" (*AP* 7).

60. Aelius Aristides, *In Defense of the Four* 309, 13–17 (translation mine). Similar denunciations of Christians with bearing on the household appear in Galen (Richard Walzer, *Galen on Jews and Christians*, p. 15) and in Celsus (Origen, *Against Celsus* 3, 55).

61. For a judicious discussion of cynicism, see Abraham J. Malherbe, "Cynics," *The Interpreter's Dictionary of the Bible*, Supplementary Volume, pp. 201–203.

62. Lucian, *The Passing of Peregrinus* 13. For other evidence identifying Christians with Cynics, see Hippolytus on Tatian (*Refutation of All Heresies* 10, 18), and the story of Serapion Arsinöites in Palladius (*Lausiac History* 37, p. 109, Butler).

63. Eph. 2:19; 1 Peter 1:1, 17; 2:11; Polycarp, *Philippians* incipit; *Martyrdom of Polycarp* incipit.

64. See William Mitchell Ramsay, *The Cities and Bishoprics of Phrygia*, 2.722.

65. Eusebius, *Ecclesiastical History* 5, 1, 20.

66. Athenagoras, *A Plea Regarding Christians* 1, 2, and 11, *Epistle to Diognetus* 5.

67. Tertullian, *Apology* 39; cf. Minucius Felix, *Octavius* 9, 2; 31, 8, and *Martyrdom of Carpus, Papylus, and Agathonice* 28–32. Abraham J. Malherbe provides a discussion of interpretations of this language in *Social Aspects of Early Christianity*, p. 40n.26.

68. E. R. Dodds, *Pagan and Christian in an Age of Anxiety: Some Aspects of Religious Experience from Marcus Aurelius to Constantine*, pp. 134–138, and Arthur Darby Nock, *Conversion: The Old and the New in Religion from Alexander the Great to Augustine of Hippo*, pp. 187–211.

69. See pp. 39–40 and 73–76.

70. Aristides, *Apology* 15:7–9.

71. Ramsay, *Cities and Bishoprics of Phrygia*, 1.2.498.

72. Ibid., 1.2.536.

73. Ibid., 1.2.530–533.

74. Jérôme Carcopino, *Daily Life in Ancient Rome: The People and the City at the Height of the Empire*, ed. by Henry T. Rowell; trans. by E. O. Lorimer, pp. 90–100.

75. Numa Denis Fustel de Coulanges, *The Ancient City: A Study on the Religion, Laws, and Institutions of Greece and Rome*, trans. by Willard Small, p. 50.

76. Ignatius, *Ephesians* 1:3.

77. Pliny, *Letters* 10, 96.

78. Ignatius, *Polycarp* 4:3.

79. The paraphrase of the story in the *Life and Miracles of St. Thecla* captures the sentiment perfectly. Thecla's relatives mourn her going after "a stranger, a charlatan, and a vagabond," and thereby "ruining the former happiness of the home" (Dagron, pp. 182–183). The martyrdom of Perpetua and Felicitas contains a document that was written by Perpetua herself and that illustrates the pathos of a pagan whose daughter's faithfulness to the church exceeds that to her family, even to her nursing son.

80. *Acts of Thomas* 59.

81. *Acts of Peter* 21, 22, 28, and 20. *Acts of Peter* 2 also mentions "two women in the lodging-house *of the Bithynians* and four who could no longer go out of their house" (singular!).

82. Sozomen, *Ecclesiastical History* 5, 15, 5.

83. *AP* 4.

84. Rosemary Radford Ruether, "Mothers of the Church: Ascetic Women in the Late Patristic Age," in *Women of Spirit: Female Leadership in the Jewish and Christian Traditions*, ed. by Rosemary Ruether and Eleanor McLaughlin, p. 73.

85. Rosemary Radford Ruether, "Misogynism and Virginal Feminism in the Fathers of the Church," in *Religion and Sexism: Images of Woman in the Jewish and Christian Traditions*, ed. by Rosemary Radford Ruether, pp. 159–160.

86. Translation mine. The text of the encomium appears in *PG* 50, col. 747.

87. Ruether, "Mothers of the Church," p. 74.

88. Ibid., p. 75.

CHAPTER III. The Pastoral Epistles Against "Old Wives' Tales"

1. It is impossible to harmonize the biographical data of the letters with Paul's undisputed letters and Acts without positing a release from his Roman imprisonment and a missionary tour to the east (to Crete, Ephesus, Macedonia, and Nicopolis) for which there is not a shred of external evidence. Furthermore, the style, vocabulary, theology, polemical devices (e.g., rhetorical denunciations and appeals to tradition), and hierarchical ecclesiastical leadership also tell against authenticity. See Werner Georg Kümmel, *Introduction to the New Testament*, 14th rev. ed. trans. by A. J. Mattill, Jr., pp. 258–272, and Martin Dibelius and Hans Conzelmann, *The Pastoral Epistles*, trans. by Philip Buttolph and Adela Yarbro (Collins), pp. 1–5.

2. The earliest witnesses to the Pastoral Epistles are Tatian (according to a note in the preface to Jerome's *Commentary on Titus*), Theophilus of Antioch (*To Autolycus* 3, 14), and perhaps Athenagoras of Athens (*A Plea Regarding Christians* 37).

3. Hans von Campenhausen, *Polykarp von Smyrna und die Pastoralbriefe*, Sitzungsberichte der Heidelberger Akademie der Wissenschaft, Philosophisch-historische Klasse, and in *Aus der Frühzeit des Christentums*, pp. 197–252.

4. The Achilles' heel of Von Campenhausen's hypothesis has to do with why Polycarp would have written under a pseudonym. He was perhaps the most widely respected bishop in Asia in the first half of the second century. He had sat

at the feet of John the Elder, was lauded by Ignatius and Irenaeus, represented the interests of Asian Christians in Rome during the Quartodeciman controversy, and after his martyrdom he was mourned and his bones venerated. His letter to the Philippians resonates with the authority of a Pauline letter. Obviously, Polycarp did not need to write pseudonymously to be heard. It is also difficult to square Polycarp's authorship of the Pastoral Epistles with his claim that he cannot compare with Paul (*Philippians* 3, 2).

5. C. F. D. Moule, "The Problem of the Pastoral Epistles: A Reappraisal," *BJRL* 47 (1964–65):430–452; August Strobel, "Schreiben des Lukas? Zum sprachlichen Problem der Pastoralbriefe," *NTS* 15 (1968–69):191–210; and Stephen G. Wilson, *Luke and the Pastoral Epistles*.

6. According to Wilson, "Luke" could have written the Pastoral Epistles if the following conditions apply: (1) if he were not Luke, Paul's companion; (2) if he wrote Acts first; (3) if after writing Acts he learned of Romans, 1 and 2 Corinthians, and fragments of other Pauline letters; and (4) if he then became concerned about Gnostic interpretations of Paul and wrote the Pastorals to refute them.

7. Horst R. Balz, "Anonymität und Pseudepigraphie im Urchristentum. Überlegungen zum literarischen und theologischen Problem der urchristlichen und gemeinantiken Pseudepigraphie," *ZTK* 66 (1969):403–436.

8. See the work by Wolfgang Speyer: *Die literarische Fälschung im heidnischen und christlichen Altertum. Ein Versuch ihrer Deutung*, Handbuch der Altertumswissenschaft 1, and his article "Religiöse Pseudepigraphie und literarische Fälschung im Altertum," JAC 8–9 (1965–66):88–125.

9. Joseph A. Sint, *Pseudonymität im Altertum. Ihre Formen und ihre Gründe*, Commentationes Aenipontanae 15.

10. Friedrich Torm, *Die Psychologie der Pseudonymität im Hinblick auf die Literatur des Urchristentums*, Studien der Luther-Akademie 2.

11. Kurt Aland, "The Problem of Anonymity and Pseudonymity in Christian Literature of the First Two Centuries," *JTS*, n.s. 12 (1961):44–45.

12. Harald Hagermann, "Der geschichtliche Ort der Pastoralbriefe," *Theologische Versuche* 2 (1970):47–64.

13. Norbert Brox, "Zum Problemstand in der Erforschung der altchristlichen Pseudepigraphie," *Kairos* 15 (1973):10–23; "Zur pseudepigraphischen Rahmung des ersten Petrusbriefes," *BZ* 19 (1975):78–96; "Pseudo-Paulus und Pseudo-Ignatius. Einige Topoi altchristlicher Pseudepigraphie," *VC* 30 (1976):181–188; and *Falsche Verfasserangaben. Zur Erklärung der frühchristlichen Pseudepigraphie*, SBS 79. Peter Trummer has attempted to unlock the mysteries of the Pastorals by using this interpretation of pseudonymity as his key (*Die Paulustradition der Pastoralbriefe*, BEvt 8).

14. Fifty-two verses out of two hundred and forty-two. The passages against false teachers are 1 Tim. 1:3–11; 4:1–5, 7–8; 6:3–10, 20; 2 Tim. 2:14–19, 23; 3:1–9; 4:3–4; Titus 1:10–16; 3:8–9.

15. Robert J. Karris, "The Background and Significance of the Polemic of the Pastoral Epistles," *JBL* 92 (1973):549–564.

16. Kümmel, *Introduction to the New Testament*, p. 267.

17. John J. Gunther, *St. Paul's Opponents and Their Background: A Study of Apocalyptic and Jewish Sectarian Teachings*, Novum Testamentum, Supplement 35, p. 4.

18. Martin Rist, "Pseudepigraphic Refutations of Marcionism," *JR* 22 (1942):39–62.

19. Tertullian, *Exhortation to Chastity* 10.

20. Epiphanius *Panarion* 49, 2. This identification of virginity with prophecy, of course, was no innovation by Montanists and Quintillians. The author of Luke-Acts emphasizes the celibacy of the widow Anna, an octogenarian Jewish prophetess (Luke 2:26–38), and the virginity of Philip's four prophesying daughters (Acts 21:8–9). Likewise, John the Seer, the author of the book of Revelation, says that itinerant prophets are those "who have not defiled themselves with women, for they are virgins' (Rev. 14:4–5). Because Codex Alexandrinus and a few other manuscripts do not contain this passage, several scholars have doubted its authenticity. I am convinced it is authentic, but even if it is not, it must be traced back to the second century, for it already appears in Chester Beatty Papyrus p[47] (third century) and verse four is quoted in *The Martyrs of Lyons and Vienne* written in 177 (Eusebius, *Ecclesiastical History* 5, 1, 10). Virginity also was a requirement for prophetesses in the Greek world.

21. For example, see Dibelius and Conzelmann, *Pastoral Epistles*, p. 69.

22. Even though the canonical Acts mentions an Alexander in Ephesus, he is not a coppersmith and does not oppose Paul. In fact, he attempts to defend Paul before a hostile mob and to vindicate the refusal of Jews and Christians to worship idols (Acts 19:33–34).

23. See p. 23.

24. In addition to these similarities, one could also mention those between Paul's friends in the *Acts of Paul* who have names similar to some in the Pastorals: Zeno and Zenas (*AP* 3:2; Titus 3:13), Artemon and Artemas (*AP* 10; Titus 3:12), Claudius and Claudia (*AP* 10; 2 Tim. 4:21), and Eubula and Eubulus (*AP* 7; 2 Tim. 4:21). None of these names appear in Paul's own letters or in Acts.

25. Ambrosiaster, in *PL* 17, col. 491. The Latin text and a French translation appear in Vouaux, *Actes*, 41.

26. Minuscule 181.

27. For example, Harnack, *Geschichte der altchristlichen Literatur bis Eusebius*, Part 2, *Die Chronologie*, 2d ed. 1.498; Carl Schlau, *Die Acten des Paulus und die ältere Thekla-Legende. Ein Beitrag zur christlichen Literaturgeschichte*, pp. 82–84; Schmidt and Schubart, *Praxeis Paulou*, 108–112; Vouaux, *Actes*, 123–124; Hennecke and Schneemelcher (eds.), *New Testament Apocrypha*, 2.348; and Johannes Rohde, "Pastoralbriefe und Acta Pauli," in *SE* 5, ed. by F. L. Cross, TU 103, pp. 303–310. Even William Ramsay, who claimed that behind the *Acts of Paul* lay a historically reliable first-century document narrating the story of Thecla, attributed the similarities by a reediting of the Thecla document sometime between 130 and 150 by someone who knew the Pastorals ("The Acta of Paul and Thekla," in *The Church in the Roman Empire Before A.D. 170*, pp. 416–417).

28. Richard Adelbert Lipsius, *Die apokryphen Apostelgeschichten und Apostellegenden. Ein Beitrag zur altchristlichen Literaturgeschichte*, 2.1.463. See also Schlau, *Acten*, pp. 83–84.

29. Peter Corssen, "Die Urgestalt der Paulusakten," *ZNW* 4 (1903):42.

30. Lipsius, *Apostelgeschichten* 2.1.461–463; Corssen, "Urgestalt," 22–47; Ramsay, "The Acta of Paul and Thekla," pp. 375–428; Salamon Reinach, "Thékla," *Annales du Musée Guimet* 35 (1910):103–140; and Wendland, *Die urchristlichen Literaturformen*, p. 338.

31. Reinach, "Thékla," 136.

32. Hans Helmut Mayer, *Über die Pastoralbriefe*, FRLANT.

33. Ibid., pp. 70–74.

34. Rohde, "Pastoralbriefe und Acta Pauli."

35. David E. Bynum, *The Daemon in the Wood: A Study of Oral Narrative Patterns*, Publications of the Milman Parry Collection, Monograph Series 1, p. 19.

36. Rohde, "Pastoralbriefe und Acta Pauli," p. 306.

37. Werner Stenger seems to have been the first to have used the phrase "die doppelte Pseudonymität" ("Timotheus und Titus als literarische Gestalten (Beobachtungen zur Form und Funktion der Pastoralbriefe)," *Kairos* 16 [1974]:252–267).

38. For a fascinating treatment of 2 Timothy as a final testament, see Otto Knoch, *Die "Testamente" des Petrus und Paulus: Die Sicherung der apostolischen Überlieferung in der Spätneutestamentlichen Zeit.*

39. But see 2 Tim. 4:21 where several other people seem to be with him in Rome.

40. Dibelius and Conzelmann, *Pastoral Epistles*, p. 38.

41. Tertullian, *Apology* 30, and Justin Martyr, *First Apology* 1, 17, 3. Notice also that contemporary Jews interpreted their offerings for pagan authorities as signs of loyalty (Aristeas, *Letter of Aristeas* 45; Josephus, *Jewish War* 2, 197, 408ff.; and Philo, *The Embassy to Gaius* 157, 317).

42. Stenger, "Timotheus und Titus," p. 267.

43. The depiction of Timothy seems to have been shaped from a reading of 1 Cor. 4:16–17; 16:10–11; and Phil. 2:19–22. Twice in these passages and four times in the Pastorals, Timothy is called Paul's child (*teknon;* 1 Cor. 4:17; Phil. 2:22; 1 Tim. 1:2, 18; 2 Tim. 1:2; 2:1). Once in the Pastorals this word *teknon* is modified by *gnēsios*, "true," which is cognate to *gnēsiōs*, "genuinely," in Phil. 2:20. From 1 Cor. 16:10–11 it appears that Timothy is shy or anxious about his mission to Corinth, and Paul asks that the Corinthians put him at ease and not despise him. So also in the Pastorals, Timothy is encouraged to be strong, courageous, and resolute (1 Tim. 6:12; 2 Tim. 1:6–7; 2:1–6), and not to let anyone despise him (1 Tim. 4:12).

The author's selection of Timothy as the primary recipient of his pseudonymous epistles no doubt is due to the unique intimacy that Timothy apparently enjoyed with Paul. He is Paul's child. No one is his equal in caring for the church (Phil. 2:20). Paul sent him to Corinth as his representative for transmitting the message that Paul had taught "everywhere in the church" (1 Cor. 4:17). In fact, by heeding Timothy the Corinthians will be assisted in imitating Paul (4:16). Both in Paul's own letters and in the Pastorals, Timothy is Paul's clone, or younger double.

But why Titus? Even though Titus appears in two of the legends behind the *Acts of Paul,* it is unlikely that the motivation for selecting him as the recipient of a letter was his appearance in the legends. As with Timothy, Titus probably was selected because of the role he plays in Paul's writings, such as in 2 Corinthians where he is mentioned eight times. Here he is depicted as an intimate companion to Paul (2 Cor. 2:13; 7:6, 13, 14), as one who cares deeply for the church (8:16–18), and as one whom Paul trusts enough to receive the Corinthians' gift for the church in Jerusalem (8:6). Paul calls Titus his partner and fellow worker (8:23), and one who walks in the same spirit and in the same footprints (12:18). No one in Paul's letters seems to have had closer ties with the apostle than Timothy and Titus.

44. Dibelius and Conzelmann cite Onosander's qualifications for a general: "I believe, then, that we must choose a general, not because of noble birth as priests are chosen, nor because of wealth as the superintendents of the gymnasia, but because he is temperate (*sōphrona*), self-restrained (*egkratē*), vigilant, frugal, hardened to labor, alert, free from avarice (*aphilargyron*), neither too young nor too old, indeed a father of children if possible, a ready speaker, and a man with a good reputation" (*Pastoral Epistles,* p. 158). Compare this passage with 1 Tim. 3:3–7 and Titus 1:7–8.

45. 1 Tim. 3:7.

46. 1 Tim. 5:14.

47. Bishops in 1 Tim. 3:2 and Titus 1:7; presbyters in Titus 1:6; deacons in 1 Tim. 3:9–10; and widows in 1 Tim. 5:6, 7, 10.

48. Bishops in 1 Tim. 3:2 and Titus 1:8; and widows in 1 Tim. 5:10.

49. 1 Tim. 3:2 and Titus 1:8; cf. Titus 2:2.

50. 1 Tim. 3:4, 8, and 11.

51. Werner Foerster, "*Eusebeia* in den Pastoralbriefen," *NTS* 5 (1958–59):216.

52. 1 Tim. 5:8.

53. This is precisely Paul's own argument in Philemon 16.

54. The word translated by the RSV as "contentment" (1 Tim. 6:6) is *autarkeia*, "the favorite virtue of the Stoics and Cynics" (Dibelius and Conzelmann, *Pastoral Epistles,* p. 84). In Stoic sources it was precisely content with the minimum of external goods that allowed the Stoic slave to consider himself wealthy and a king. For example, Stobaeus wrote: "Contentment is nature's wealth" (*Eclogae* 3; p. 265, 13, Hense). Epictetus is recorded to have said: "The art of living well . . . is contingent upon moderation, and contentment, orderliness, propriety, and thrift" (according to Stobaeus this appeared in the *Gnomology*).

55. Ignatius, *Polycarp* 4:3.

56. In addition to those passages already cited one might list Col. 3:22; 4:1; Eph. 6:5–9; and 1 Peter 2:18–20.

57. 1 Tim. 5:11–12.

58. 1 Tim. 5:12.

59. 1 Tim. 5:16.

60. 1 Tim. 5:5, 10, 13.

61. Ignatius, *Smyrneans* 12.

62. 1 Tim. 5:4, 8, 9, 10, and 16.

63. See pp. 50–53, 95.

64. See p. 39-40, 111 n. 39.

65. 1 Tim. 1:20 (6:3–5); 2 Tim. 4:14–15; Titus 3:8–11.

66. 1 Tim. 4:7. Cf. 2 Tim. 4:4, where the author complains about those who "will turn away from listening to the truth and wander into myths."

CHAPTER IV. The Victory of the Pastoral Epistles

1. David L. Balch has shown that these instructions "concerning household management" in 1 Peter were intended to counteract reactions against the church as socially disruptive, especially to the household. He also argues that tension between Christians and pagans in Asia Minor was not primarily political but social (*Let Wives Be Submissive: The Domestic Code in 1 Peter,* Society of Biblical Literature, Monograph Series 26). Elliot also treats the crisis of the household in 1 Peter in great detail (*A Home for the Homeless*).

2. If Pierre Prigent is correct, the bishops were not the most conciliatory faction of the church in Asia, for, he claims, the heretics opposed by Ignatius preached that "it is not necessary to risk one's life to avoid compromise with paganism; martyrdom is not a Christian vocation" ("Hérésie asiate et l'église confessante: De l'Apocalypse à Ignace," *VC* 31 [1977]:22).

3. For an authoritative discussion of Montanism, see Pierre Champagne de Labriolle, *La Crise Montaniste*.

4. See G. Nathaniel Bonwetsch, *Die Geschichte des Montanismus*, pp. 108–118.

5. Montanus according to Tertullian (*On Flight in Persecution* 9).

6. Eusebius, *Ecclesiastical History* 5, 18, 2.

7. According to Apollonius in Eusebius, *Ecclesiastical History* 5, 18, 3.

8. Tertullian, *Against Valentinians* 5.

9. Bonwetsch, *Die Geschichte des Montanismus*, p. 149. See also Wilhelm E. Schlepelern, *Der Montanismus und die phrygischen Kulte. Eine religionsgeschichtliche Untersuchung*, trans. by W. Bauer.

10. As Tertullian rightly emphasized. See, for example, *On Monogamy* 1.

11. Tertullian, *Against Praxeas* 1.

12. Apollonius in Eusebius, *Ecclesiastical History* 5, 18, 13 and 14.

13. According to a letter of Serapion of Antioch in Eusebius, *Ecclesiastical History* 5, 19, 3.

14. Eusebius, *Ecclesiastical History* 5, 16, 3 and 4.

15. Philip Carrington, *The Early Christian Church*, Vol 2.: *The Second Christian Century*, pp. 182–183.

16. Eusebius, *Ecclesiastical History* 5, 16, 8.

17. Ibid., 5, 18, 5.

18. Ibid., 6, 20, 3.

19. Ibid., 5, 16, 17.

20. Ibid., 5, 17, 1.

21. I cannot agree with H. Paulsen that Montanism had no formative effect on the New Testament canon ("Die Bedeutung des Montanismus für die Herausbildung des Kanons," *VC* 32 [1978]:19–52).

22. Eusebius, *Ecclesiastical History* 3, 28, 1–5.

23. Ibid., 7, 25, 1–4.

24. Ibid., 3, 25, 2–4.

25. Ibid., 3, 39, 14.

26. Maximus, Oecumenius, Andreas Caesariensis, and Anastasius Sinaita (see ANF 1.153–155).

27. Eusebius, *Ecclesiastical History* 3, 39, 12.

28. Ibid., 3, 39, 13.

29. Irenaeus, *Against Heresies* 5, 32.

30. Ibid., 3, 11, 9.

31. In the year 177, before Irenaeus arrived in Gaul, the churches in Lyons and neighboring Vienne wrote a letter describing the horrible persecutions against Christians in Gaul, and it is addressed to the believers in Asia and Phrygia, "who have the same faith and hope of redemption as ourselves" (Eusebius, *Ecclesiastical History* 5, 1, 3). One of the martyrs originally had come from Phrygia years before and was known for his glossolalia. Irenaeus' appointment as bishop of Lyons itself suggests a strong relationship between Gaul and Asia Minor. Notice also that the letter contains three allusions to the Apocalypse of John, revealing the importance of the book in those churches.

32. Pp. 63–64.

33. Tertullian, *Against Marcion* 5, 21, 1.

34. Jerome's *Commentary on Titus* (*PL* 29, cols. 589–590). See also Clement of Alexandria, *Stromateis* 2, 52, 5–7.

35. Tertullian, *On Monogamy* 15. Origen uses this text against Montanists in *On First Principles* 2, 7, 3. See also Theodoret, *Compendium of Heretical Fables* 3, 2, and Timothy of Constantinople, *On the Reception of Heretics* (*PG* 86, 1, col. 20).

36. Tertullian, *On Fasting* 15.

37. John Strugnell, "A Plea for Conjectural Emendation in the New Testament, with a Coda on 1 Cor 4:6," *CBQ* 34 (1974):543–558.

38. MacDonald, "A Conjectural Emendation of 1 Cor 15:31–32," *HTR* 73 (1980):265–276.

39. William O. Walker, Jr., gives a good summary of the arguments and bibliography for 1 Cor. 14:33b–36 being an interpolation in "1 Corinthians 11:2–16 and Paul's Views Regarding Women," *JBL* 94 (1975):95,n.6.

40. Surely this was the motivation behind the interpolation in 1 Cor. 15:31.

CHAPTER V. The Victory of the Legends

1. Origen, *Commentary on the Gospel of St. John* 20, 12, and *On First Principles* 1, 2, 3.

2. Hennecke and Schneemelcher (eds.), *New Testament Apocrypha* 2.178–188. See also *A Manichaean Psalm-Book*, Vol. 2, ed. and tr. by C. R. C. Allberry, Manichaean Manuscripts of the Chester Beatty Collection 2, p. 143, lines 4–10.

3. Hennecke and Schneemelcher (eds.), *New Testament Apocrypha* 2.324.

4. Oskar Leopold von Gebhardt, *Passio sanctae Theclae virginis: die lateinischen Übersetzungen der Acta Pauli et Theclae*, TU n.s. 7, 2.

5. *Dictionary of Christian Biography* 4.895.

6. Ibid., 885. Concerning the popularity of the *Acts of Paul and Thecla*, see also Leclercq, *Les Martyrs*, Vol. 1: *Les Temps Néroniens et le deuxième siècle*, pp. 141–142 and 151.

7. Hennecke and Schneemelcher (eds.), *New Testament Apocrypha* 2.346.

8. Ibid.

9. For a discussion of the transmission of the *Martyrdom of Paul*, see Lipsius and Bonnet (eds.), *Acta apostolorum apocrypha* 1. xxiii–xxxiii and lv–lvii.

10. See a discussion of a parallel phenomenon in modern Yugoslavia in Lord, *The Singer of Tales*, pp. 124–138.

11. Methodius, *Symposium*, Discourse 11, ch. 1.

12. Ibid., ch. 2.

13. Gregory of Nyssa, *Life of Macrina* 2.

14. Gregory of Nyssa, *Homily 14 on the Song of Songs;* Gregory of Nazianzus, *Oration Against Julian* I, 69.

15. *Dictionary of Christian Biography* 4.887.

16. Baronius, *Martyrologium romanum*, p. 434.

17. John Chrysostom, *Homily 25 on the Acts of the Apostles* 4. Pseudo-Chrysostom, *A Panegyric to Thecla,* wrongly attributed to Chrysostom, probably was written not long afterward.

18. It is most interesting to see how Chrysostom treats 1 Timothy 5 where the author tries to shrink the order of widows. In Constantinople there were two separate orders for celibate women: virgins and widows. Chrysostom applies the

passage only to widows, and interprets "Paul's" silence concerning the virgins to prove the apostle's great esteem for them. "Paul having discoursed much concerning widows, and having settled the age at which they were to be admitted ... proceeds now to say, 'But the younger widows refuse.' But concerning virgins, though the case of their falling is a much more gross one, he has said nothing of this kind, and rightly. For they had enrolled themselves on higher views, and the work with them proceeded from a greater elevation of mind. Therefore the receiving of strangers, and the washing of the Saints' feet, he has represented by 'attending upon the Lord without distraction,' and by saying, 'The unmarried careth for the things that belong to the Lord.' And if he has not limited a particular age for them it is most likely because that point is settled by what he has said in this case. But indeed, as I said, the choice of virginity proceeded from a higher purpose. Besides, in this case there had been falls, and thus they had given occasion for his rule, but nothing of that kind had occurred among the virgins" (Chrysostom, *Homily 15 on 1 Timothy* 1; the translation comes from *NPNF* first series 13.459).

19. *Dictionary of Christian Biography* 4.894.

20. Monumenta Asiae Minoris Antiqua, III:45, 102; and Gustave Lefebvre (ed.), *Recueil des inscriptions grecques chrétiennes d'Égypte* (Cairo: L'Institute Français d'Archéologie Orientale, 1907), p. 692.

21. *DACL* 7., col. 1971, fig. 6038.

22. Monumenta Asiae Minoris Antiqua I:209, 231, 325, 327, 334, 358, 383; III:45, 128, 161, 372, 411a, 486, 532, 576, 664, 700; V:77; VII:71, 74, 104, 567, 578, 581; Basil, *Letters* 321; and *Life and Miracles of St. Thecla*, mir. 11.

23. *Dictionary of Christian Biography* 4.897.

24. Gregory of Nazianzus, *On the Great Athanasius* 22.

25. Ernest E. Herzfeld and Samuel Guyer, *Meriamlik und Korykos, zwei christliche Ruinenstätten des Rauhen Kilikiens*, Monumenta Asiae Minoris Antiqua II.

26. The critical Greek text and a French translation appear in an encyclopedic edition by Gilbert Dagron, *Vie et miracles de sainte Thècle*, Subsidia Hagiographica 62.

27. Egeria, *Travels* 23, 1–6, as translated by John Wilkinson in *Egeria's Travels*, pp. 121–122.

28. Theodoret, *Religious History* 29.

29. "It is evident that the women made up the bulk of her clientele, and that the problems of women were her specialty" (Dagron, 100).

30. *Life and Miracles of St. Thecla*, mirs. 11, 14, 18 (which contains two stories about women), 19, 20, 21, 24, 32, 34, 42, 43, 44, 45, 46.

31. Dagron, 134.

32. *Dictionary of Christian Biography* 4.894.

33. *DACL* 2., col. 2668, fig. 2221.

34. Ibid., 1., col. 1729–1732, fig. 452, and 11., col. 386, fig. 7979.

35. Ibid., 1., col. 2577, fig. 850.

36. Ibid., 1., col. 1122–1123, fig. 273.

37. Lefebvre (ed.), *Recueil des inscriptions grecques chrétiennes d'Égypte*, p. 692.

38. *DACL* 13, col. 2967, fig. 10000.

39. Jerome, *Letter to Eustochium;* Ambrose, *Letters*, letter 63, and *Concerning Virgins* II, 3; Sulpicius Severus, *Dialogues* 2, 13, 5.

40. *Acts of Xanthippe and Polyxena* 36.

41. See pp. 91–92.

42. *Dictionary of Christian Biography* 4.896.

43. Jerome, *Chronicle* 377.

44. *Dictionary of Christian Biography* 4.896–897.

45. Ibid., 896.

46. Ibid.

47. Louis Jalabert and René Mouterde (eds.), *Inscriptions grecques et latines de la Syria,* IV:1585; V:2044; and Lefebvre (ed.), *Recueil des inscriptions grecques chrétiennes d'Égypte* 84, 96, 101, 107, 108, 420, 574, and 670.

48. *Dictionary of Christian Biography* 4.897.

49. However, there is evidence that Manichaeans too used the Pastorals. According to Archelaus, Mani quoted 1 Tim. 1:20 in his defense (*Disputation with Manes* 13).

50. Augustine, *Reply to Faustus* 30:4, NPNF first series 4.328–329.

51. Ibid., 30:6.

52. Ibid.

53. This chapter by no means exhausts the evidence for Thecla's popularity. See in addition Epiphanius, *Panarion* 47, 1–2; Nicetas Paphlago, *Oration 16 in Praise of St. Thecla;* (Pseudo?) Photius, *Panegyric to the Holy Protomartyr Thecla;* and the evidence cited by Gebhardt, *Passio sanctae Theclae virginis: die lateinischen Übersetzung der Acta Pauli et Theclae,* TU 7, 2.169–182, and by Ernest Lucius, *Die Anfänge des Heiligenkults in der christlichen Kirche,* ed. by Gustave Anrich, pp. 205–214. We also have evidence that the legend about Paul and the baptized lion also continued to be told. See Hippolytus, *Commentary on Daniel* 3, 29; Commodian, *Carmen Apologeticum adversus Judaeos et Gentes* 627–628; the *Acts of Titus* 6; and the *Epistle of Pelagia.*

CONCLUSION

1. For an excellent discussion of the complexity of Paul's attitudes toward society, see J. Christiaan Beker, *Paul the Apostle: The Triumph of God in Life and Thought,* pp. 303–327.

2. Wayne A. Meeks, "The Christian Proteus," in *The Writings of St. Paul,* ed. by Wayne A. Meeks, pp. 435–444. The passage in the *Odyssey* treating Proteus is 4:383–570.

3. Some interpreters have argued that Paul did nothing more than ask Philemon to accept Onesimus back with impunity for having run away, and they use 1 Cor. 7:24 as proof that Paul condoned slavery. In vs. 20–21 he says: "Every one should remain in the state in which he was called. Were you a slave when called? Never mind." But the passage immediately following (vs. 25–31) shows that Paul instructed slaves to be content because one's present status—be it social, marital, or financial—already was relativized by the nearness of Christ's coming: "the appointed time has grown very short" (v. 29a). Furthermore, he encourages slaves to gain their freedom if they have the chance (v. 21), and forbids Christians to become slaves (v. 23).

4. From jail Paul wrote the Philippians that even though other missionaries were creating their own circles of followers in order to make Paul's imprisonment even more painful, he did not mind as long as the gospel succeeded: "Whether in pretense or in truth, Christ is proclaimed; and in that I rejoice" (Phil. 1:18).

5. The letters are: (1) Phil. 4:10–20; (2) Phil. 1:3 to 3:1; 4:4–9, 21–23; and (3) Phil. 3:2 to 4:3.

6. Compare 1 Cor. 4:17 and 2 Tim. 1:2; 1 Cor. 5:5 and 1 Tim. 1:20; 1 Cor. 9:9 and 1 Tim. 5:18; 1 Cor. 9:25 and 2 Tim. 2:5 and 4:8; 1 Cor. 15:9 and 1 Tim. 1:16; 1 Cor. 16:5–11 and 1 Tim. 1:3.

BIBLIOGRAPHY

SOURCES AND TRANSLATIONS

Acts of John. Translated by Knut Schäferdiek. *New Testament Apocrypha* 2.215–258.

Acts of Paul. Translated by Wilhelm Schneemelcher. *New Testament Apocrypha* 2.352–387. Appendix translated by R. Kasser, 387–390.

Acts of Peter. Translated by Wilhelm Schneemelcher. *New Testament Apocrypha* 2.276–322.

Acts of Philip. Translated by Montague Rhodes James. *The Apocryphal New Testament,* 439–453.

Acts of Thomas. Translated by Günther Bornkamm. *New Testament Apocrypha* 2.442–531.

Acts of Titus. Translation appears in Montague Rhodes James. *JTS* 6 (1905):549–556.

Acts of Xanthippe and Polyxena. Translated by W. A. Craigie. ANF supplement (Vol. 10). 205–217.

Ambrose. *Concerning Virgins.* Translated by H. de Romestin. NPNF second series 10.363–387.

———. *Letters* 63. Translated by H. de Romestin. NPNF second series 10.457–473.

Ambrosiaster. Text appears in *PL* 17.4–582.

Apocalypse of Paul. Translated by Hugo Duensing. *New Testament Apocrypha* 2.759–798.

Apuleius. *The Golden Ass.* Translated by Robert Graves. *The Golden Ass of Apuleius.* Pocket Library, 1954.

Archelaus. *Disputation with Manes.* Translated by S. D. F. Salmond. ANF 6.179–252.

Aristeas. *Letter of Aristeas.* Translated by Moses Hadas. *Aristeas to Philocrates.* Harper & Brothers, 1951.

Aristides. *Apology.* Translated by D. M. Kay. ANF supplement (Vol. 10). 263–279.

Aristides, Aelius. *In Defense of the Four.* Text edited by Wilhelm Dindorf. *Aristides.* 3 vols. Leipzig: G. Reimer, 1829.

Athenagoras. *A Plea Regarding Christians.* Edited and translated by Cyril C. Richardson. *Early Christian Fathers,* 300–340. Library of Christian Classics 1. Westminster Press, 1953.

Augustine. *Reply to Faustus.* Translated by Richard Stothert. NPNF first series 4.155–345.

Baronius, Cesare. *Martyrologium romanum.* Venice, 1593.

Basil. *Letters.* Text and translation by Roy J. Deferrari and M. R. P. McGuire. St. Basil. *The Letters* 4. Loeb.

Canon Muratori. Text appears in F. W. Grosheide. *Some Early Lists of the Books of the New Testament,* 5–11. Textus minores 1. Leiden: E. J. Brill, 1948.

Chrysostom, John. *Homily 15 on 1 Timothy.* Translated by James Tweed. NPNF first series 13.459–464.

————. *Homily 25 on the Acts of the Apostles.* Translated by J. Walker, J. Sheppard, H. Browne, and George B. Stevens. NPNF first series 11.162–167.

Cicero. *On the Nature of the Gods.* Text and translation by H. Rackham. *Cicero* 19. Loeb.

Clement of Alexandria. *Stromateis.* Translated by W. Wilson. ANF 2.299–567.

Clement of Rome. *1 Clement.* Text and translation by Kirsopp Lake. *The Apostolic Fathers* 1.8–121. Loeb.

Commodian. *Carmen Apologeticum adversus Judaeos et Gentes.* Text appears in B. Dombart, CSEL 15.

Correspondence Between Seneca and Paul. Translated by Alfons Kurfess. *New Testament Apocrypha* 2.135–141.

Cyprian. *Epistles.* Translated by Ernest Wallis. ANF 5.275–409.

Didache. Text and translation by Kirsopp Lake. *The Apostolic Fathers* 1.308–333. Loeb.

Didymus the Blind. *On the Trinity.* Text appears in *PG* 39, cols. 131–1818.

Dio Cassius. *Roman History.* Text and translation by Earnest Cary. *Dio's Roman History.* 9 vols. Loeb.

Dio Chrysostom. *Discourses.* Text and translation by J. W. Cohoon. *Dio Chrysostom* 1. Loeb.

Egeria. *Travels.* Translated by John Wilkinson. *Egeria's Travels.* London: S.P.C.K., 1971.

Epiphanius. *Panarion.* Text appears in *PG* 41–43.

Epistle of Pelagia. Translated by Edgar J. Goodspeed. *The Epistle of Pelagia.* University of Chicago Press, 1931.

Epistle to Diognetus. Text and translation by Kirsopp Lake. *The Apostolic Fathers* 2.350–379. Loeb.

Epistle to the Laodiceans. Translated by Wilhelm Schneemelcher. *New Testament Apocrypha* 2.131–132.

Eusebius. *Ecclesiastical History.* Text and translation by Kirsopp Lake and J. E. L. Oulton. Eusebius, *Ecclesiastical History.* 2 vols. Loeb.

Gellius, Aulus. *Attic Nights.* Text and translation by John C. Rolfe. *The Attic Nights of Aulus Gellius.* 3 vols. Loeb.

Gospel of Philip (CG II, 51, 29–86, 19). Translated by Wesley W. Isenberg. *The Nag Hammadi Library in English,* 131–151.

Gospel of Thomas (CG II, 32, 10–51, 29). Translated by Thomas O. Lambdin. *The Nag Hammadi Library in English,* 118–130.

Gregory of Nazianzus. *On the Great Athanasius.* Translated by Charles Gordon Browne and James Edward Swallow. NPNF second series 7.269–283.

———. *Oration Against Julian I.* Text appears in *PG* 35,1, cols. 532–664.

Gregory of Nyssa. *Homily 14 on the Song of Songs.* Text appears in *PG* 44, cols. 1062–1088.

———. *Life of Macrina.* Text and French translation appear in Pierre Maraval. *Vie de sainte Macrine.* SC 178.

Hippolytus. *Commentary on Daniel.* Translated by S. D. F. Salmond. ANF 5.177–191.

———. *Refutation of All Heresies.* Translated by J. H. Macmahon. ANF 5.9–153.

Horace. *Satires.* Text and translation by H. R. Fairdough. Horace. *Satires.* Loeb.

Hyginus, *Fables.* Translation appears in Mary Grant. *The Myths of Hyginus.* University of Kansas Publications, Humanistic Studies 34. University of Kansas Press, 1960.

Hypostasis of the Archons (CG II, 86, 20–97, 23). Translated by Bentley Layton. *The Nag Hammadi Library in English*, 152–160.

Ignatius. *Ephesians.* Text and translation by Kirsopp Lake. *The Apostolic Fathers* 1.172–197. Loeb.

———. *Magnesians.* Text and translation by Kirsopp Lake. *The Apostolic Fathers* 1.196–211. Loeb.

———. *Philadelphians.* Text and translation by Kirsopp Lake. *The Apostolic Fathers* 1.238–251. Loeb.

———. *Polycarp.* Text and translation by Kirsopp Lake. *The Apostolic Fathers* 1.266–277. Loeb.

———. *Romans.* Text and translation by Kirsopp Lake. *The Apostolic Fathers* 1.224–239. Loeb.

———. *Smyrneans.* Text and translation by Kirsopp Lake. *The Apostolic Fathers* 1.250–267. Loeb.

———. *Trallians.* Text and translation by Kirsopp Lake. *The Apostolic Fathers* 1.212–225. Loeb.

Irenaeus. *Against Heresies.* Translated by Alexander Roberts et al. ANF 1.315–578.

Jerome. *Chronicle.* See J. K. Fotheringham, ed. *Eusebii Pamphili chronici canones.* London: Humphrey Milford, 1923.

———. *Commentary on Titus, Preface.* Text appears in *PL* 29, cols. 589–590.

———. *Letter to Eustochium* (22). Translated by W. H. Fremantle. NPNF second series 6.22–41.

———. *On Illustrious Men.* Translated by Ernest Cushing Richardson. NPNF second series 3.359–384.

Josephus. *The Jewish War.* Text and translation by H. St. J. Thackeray. Josephus. *Jewish War.* 2 vols. Loeb.

Justin Martyr. *First Apology.* Edited and translated by Edward Rochie Hardy. *Early Christian Fathers*, 242–289. Library of Christian Classics 1. Westminster Press, 1953.

Lactantius. *Divine Institutes.* Translated by Mary Francis McDonald. *Lactantius: The Divine Institutes*, books 1–7. The Fathers of the Church, A New Translation 49. Catholic University of America Press, 1964.

Life and Miracles of St. Thecla. Text and French translation appear in Gilbert Dagron. *Vie et miracles de sainte Thècle.* Subsidia Hagiographica 62. Brussels: Société des Bollandistes, 1978.

Longus. *Daphnis and Chloe.* Translated by Moses Hadas. *Three Greek Romances*, 4–68. Library of the Liberal Arts. Bobbs-Merrill Co., 1953.

Lucian. *The Lover of Lies.* Text and translation by A. M. Harmon. *Lucian* 3.319–381. Loeb.

———. *The Passing of Peregrinus.* Text and translation by A. M. Harmon. *Lucian* 5.2–51. Loeb.

A Manichaean Psalm-Book, Vol. 2. Edited and translated by C. R. C. Allberry. Manichaean Manuscripts of the Chester Beatty Collection 2. Stuttgart: W. Kohlhammer, 1938.

Martyrdom of Carpus, Papylus, and Agathonice. Text and translation by Herbert Musurillo. *The Acts of the Christian Martyrs,* 22–37. London: Oxford University Press, 1972.

Martyrdom of Paul. Translated by Wilhelm Schneemelcher. *New Testament Apocrypha* 2.383–387.

Martyrdom of Perpetua and Felicitas. Text and translation by Herbert Musurillo. *The Acts of the Christian Martyrs,* 106–131, London: Oxford University Press, 1972.

Martyrdom of Polycarp. Translated by Kirsopp Lake. *The Apostolic Fathers* 2.312–345. Loeb.

The Martyrs of Lyons and Vienne. Text and translation appear in Herbert Musurillo. *The Acts of the Christian Martyrs,* 62–85. London: Oxford University Press, 1972.

Methodius. *Symposium.* Translated by W. R. Clark. ANF 6.309–355.

Minucius Felix. *Octavius.* Text and translation by G. H. Rendall. Tertullian. *Apology,* 314–437. Loeb.

Nicephorus Callistus. *Church History.* Text appears in *PG* 145, cols. 559–1332, 146, and 147, cols. 9–448.

Nicetas Paphlago. *Oration 16 in Praise of St. Thecla.* Text appears in *PG* 105, cols. 301–336.

On the Origin of the World (CG II, 97, 24–127, 17). Translated by Hans-Gebhard Bethge and Orval S. Wintermute. *The Nag Hammadi Library in English,* 162–179.

Origen. *Against Celsus.* Translated by Henry Chadwick. *Origen: Contra Celsum.* Cambridge University Press, 1965.

———. *Commentary on the Gospel of St. John.* Translated by Allan Menzies. ANF supplement (Vol. 10). 297–408.

———. *On First Principles.* Translated by G. W. Butterworth. *Origen: On First Principles.* Peter Smith, 1973.

Ovid. *Metamorphoses.* Text and translation by Frank Justus Miller. Ovid *Metamorphoses.* 2 vols. Loeb.

Palladius. *Lausiac History.* Translated by Robert T. Meyer. *Palladius: The Lausiac History.* ACW 34. Newman Press, 1965.

Philaster of Brescia. *Book of the Heresies.* Text appears in *PL* 12, cols. 1111–1302.

Philip of Side. *Church History.* Text appears in Carl G. de Boor. *Neue Fragmente des Papias, Hegesippus und Pierius . . . aus der Kirchengeschichte des Philippus Sidetes,* 165–184. TU 5, 2. Leipzig: J. C. Hinrichs, 1888.

Philo. *The Embassy to Gaius.* Text and translation by F. H. Colson. *Philo* 10.2–187. Loeb.

Philostratus the Elder. *Imagines.* Text and translation by Arthur Fairbanks. Philostratus. *Imagines.* Loeb.

Philostratus, Flavius. *Life of Apollonius of Tyana.* Text and translation by F. C. Conybeare. Philostratus. *Life of Apollonius of Tyana.* 2 vols. Loeb.

Photius (Pseudo?). *Panegyric to the Holy Protomartyr Thecla.* Text appears in S. Aristarches. *Phōtiou logoi kai homiliai,* Vol. 2, 252–267. Constantinople: Annuaire Oriental and Printing Co., 1901.

Plato. *Gorgias.* Text and translation by W. R. M. Lamb. *Plato* 3.246–533. Loeb.

————. *Republic.* Translated by G. M. A. Grube. *Plato's Republic.* Hackett Publishing Co., 1974.

Pliny. *Letters.* Text and translation by Betty Radice. Pliny. *Letters and Panegyricus.* 2 vols. Loeb.

Polycarp. *Philippians.* Translated by Kirsopp Lake. *The Apostolic Fathers* 1.282–301. Loeb.

Prayer of the Apostle Paul (CG I, A, 1–B, 10). Translated by Dieter Mueller. *The Nag Hammadi Library in English,* 27–28.

Pseudo-Chrysostom. *Panegyric to Thecla.* Text appears in *PG* 50, cols. 745–748. See also Michel Aubineau, "Panégyrique de Thècla attribué à Jean Chrysostome (BHG 1720): La fin retrouvée d'un texte mutilé." *Analecta Bollandiana* 93 (1975):349–355.

Quintilian. *Institutes.* Text and translation by H. E. Butler. *The Institutio Oratoria of Quintilian.* 4 vols. Loeb.

Sophia of Jesus Christ (CG III, 90, 14–119, 18, and BG 8502, 128, 1–141, 7). Translated by Douglas M. Parrott. *The Nag Hammadi Library in English,* 207–228.

Sozomen. *Ecclesiastical History.* Translated by Chester D. Hartranft. NPNF second series. 239–427.

Stobaeus. *Eclogae.* Text appears in *Joannis Stobaei Anthologium.* Edited by Curtus Wachsmuth and Otto Hense. Berlin: Weidmann, 1884–1923.

Strabo. *Geography.* Text and translation by Horace L. Jones. *The Geography of Strabo.* 8 vols. Loeb.

Suetonius. *Life of Nero.* Text and translation by J. C. Rolfe. Suetonius. *The Lives of the Caesars* 2.86–187. Loeb.

Sulpicius Severus. *Dialogues.* Translated by Alexander Roberts. NPNF second series. 3–122.

Tacitus. *Histories.* Text and translation by Clifford H. Moore. Tacitus. *The Histories.* 4 vols. Loeb.

Tatian. *Oration to the Greeks.* Translated by J. E. Ryland. ANF 2.65–83.

Tertullian. *Against Marcion.* Translated by Peter Holmes. ANF 3.271–474.

————. *Against Praxeas.* Translated by Peter Holmes. ANF 3.597–627.

————. *Against Valentinians.* Translated by Peter Holmes. ANF 3.503–520.

————. *Apology.* Translated by S. Thelwall. ANF 3.17–55.

————. *The Chaplet.* Translated by S. Thelwall. ANF 3.93–103.

————. *Exhortation to Chastity.* Translated by S. Thelwall. ANF 4.50–58.

————. *On Baptism.* Translated by S. Thelwall. ANF 3.669–679.

————. *On Fasting.* Translated by S. Thelwall. ANF 4.102–114.

————. *On Flight in Persecution.* Translated by S. Thelwall. ANF 4.116–125.

————. *On Monogamy.* Translated by S. Thelwall. ANF 4.59–72.

————. *On Spectacles.* Translated by S. Thelwall. ANF 3.79–91.

————. *On the Veiling of Virgins.* Translated by S. Thelwall. ANF 4.27–37.

————. *Prescription Against Heretics.* Translated by Peter Holmes. ANF 3.243–265.

————. *To Scapula.* Translated by S. Thelwall. ANF 3.105–108.

Theodoret. *Compendium of Heretical Fables.* Text appears in *PG* 83, cols. 335–556.

_____. *Religious History.* Translated by Blomfield Jackson. NPNF second series 3.33–159.
Theophilus of Antioch. *To Autolycus.* Translated by Robert M. Grant. *Ad Autolycum.* Oxford Early Christian Texts. Oxford: Clarendon Press, 1970.
Thought of Norea (CG IX, 27, 11–29, 5). Translated by Søren Giversen and Birger A. Pearson. *The Nag Hammadi Library in English,* 404–405.
Timothy of Constantinople. *On the Reception of Heretics.* Text appears in *PG* 86 (1), cols. 11–74.

MODERN WORKS CITED

Aland, Kurt. "The Problem of Anonymity and Pseudonymity in Christian Literature of the First Two Centuries." *JTS,* n.s. 12 (1961):39–49.
Aleith, Eva. *Paulusverständis in der alten Kirche.* BZNW 18. Berlin: Töpelmann, 1937.
Allberry, C. R. C., ed. and tr. *A Manichaean Psalm-Book,* Vol. 2. Manichaean Manuscripts of the Chester Beatty Collection 2. Stuttgart: W. Kohlhammer, 1938.
Balch, David L. *Let Wives Be Submissive: The Domestic Code in 1 Peter.* Society of Biblical Literature, Monograph Series 26. Scholars Press, 1981.
Balz, Horst R. "Anonymität und Pseudepigraphie im Urchristentum. Überlegungen zum literarischen und theologischen Problem der urchristlichen und gemeinantiken Pseudepigraphie." *ZTK* 66 (1969):403–436.
Barnett, Albert E. *Paul Becomes a Literary Influence.* University of Chicago Press, 1941.
Bascom, William R. "Folklore and Anthropology." In *The Study of Folklore,* edited by Alan Dundes, pp. 25–33. Prentice-Hall, 1965.
Beker, J. Christiaan. *Paul the Apostle: The Triumph of God in Life and Thought.* Fortress Press, 1980.
Bell, Nancy R.E. *Lives and Legends of the Evangelists, Apostles, and Other Early Saints.* London: George Bell, 1901.
Bibliotheca Hagiographica Graeca, 3d ed. S.v. "Thècle."
Bonwetsch, G. Nathaniel. *Die Geschichte des Montanismus.* Erlangen: Andreas Deichart, 1881.
Brown, Raymond E. *The Community of the Beloved Disciple.* Paulist Press, 1979.
Brox, Norbert. *Falsche Verfasserangaben. Zur Erklärung der frühchristlichen Pseudepigraphie.* SBS 79. Stuttgart: KBW Verlag, 1975.
_____. "Pseudo-Paulus und Pseudo-Ignatius. Einige Topoi altchristlicher Pseudepigraphie." *VC* 30 (1976):181–188.
_____. "Zum Problemstand in der Erforschung der altchristlichen Pseudepigraphie." *Kairos* 15 (1973):10–23.
_____. "Zur pseudepigraphischen Rahmung des ersten Petrusbriefes." *BZ* 19 (1975):78–96.
Bynum, David E. *The Daemon in the Wood: A Study of Oral Narrative Patterns.* Publications of the Milman Parry Collection, Monograph Series 1. Harvard University Press, 1978.
Campenhausen, Hans von. *Aus der Frühzeit des Christentums.* Tübingen: J. C. B. Mohr (Paul Siebeck), 1963.

––––––. *The Formation of the Christian Bible.* Translated by J. A. Baker. Fortress Press, 1972.

––––––. *Polykarp von Smyrna und die Pastoralbriefe.* Sitzungsberichte der Heidelberger Akademie der Wissenschaft; Philosophisch-historische Klasse. Heidelberg: Carl Winter, 1951.

Carcopino, Jérôme. *Daily Life in Ancient Rome: The People and the City at the Height of the Empire.* Edited by Henry T. Rowell. Translated by E. O. Lorimer. Yale University Press, 1940.

Carrington, Philip. *The Early Christian Church.* Vol. 2: *The Second Christian Century.* Cambridge University Press, 1957.

Cohn, Norman. *The Pursuit of the Millennium: Revolutionary Millenarians and Mystical Anarchists of the Middle Ages.* Rev. and enl. ed. Oxford University Press, 1970.

Conybeare, F. C. *The Armenian Apology and Acts of Apollonius.* 2d ed. Macmillan, 1896.

Corssen, Peter. "Die Töchter des Philippus." *ZNW* 2 (1901):289–299.

––––––. "Die Urgestalt der Paulusakten." *ZNW* 4 (1903):22–47.

Dagron, Gilbert. *Vie et miracles de sainte Thècle.* Subsidia Hagiographica 62. Brussels: Société des Bollandistes, 1978.

Dan, Ilana. "The Innocent Persecuted Heroine: An Attempt at a Model for the Surface Level of the Narrative Structure of the Female Fairy Tale." In *Patterns in Oral Literature,* edited by Heda Jason and Dimitri Segal, pp. 13–30. World Anthropology Series. The Hague: Mouton & Co., 1977.

Dassmann, Ernst. *Der Stachel im Fleisch. Paulus in der frühchristlichen Literatur bis Irenäus.* Münster: Aschendorff, 1979.

Davies, Stevan L. *The Revolt of the Widows: The Social World of the Apocryphal Acts.* Southern Illinois University Press, 1980.

Delehaye, Hippolyte. *Die hagiographischen Legenden.* Translated by E. A. Stückelberg. Munich: J. Kösel, 1907.

Dibelius, Martin, and Conzelmann, Hans. *The Pastoral Epistles.* Translated by Philip Buttolph and Adela Yarbro (Collins). Hermeneia. Fortress Press, 1972.

Dictionary of Christian Biography. S.v. "Thecla (1)," "Thecla (2)," "Thecla (4)," "Thecla (5)," "Thecla (6)," "Thecla (7)," "Thecla (9)," "Thecla (10)," "Thecla (11)," by John Gwynn.

Dictionnaire d'archéologie chrétienne et de liturgie. S.v. "Thècle (sainte)," by H. Leclercq.

Dodds, E. R. *Pagan and Christian in an Age of Anxiety: Some Aspects of Religious Experience from Marcus Aurelius to Constantine.* Cambridge University Press, 1965. Reprint. New York: W. W. Norton & Co., 1970.

Elliot, John H. *A Home for the Homeless: A Sociological Exegesis of 1 Peter, Its Situation and Strategy.* Fortress Press, 1981.

Festugière, A. J. "Lieux Communs littéraires et thèmes de folk-lore dans l'hagiographie primitive." *Wiener Studien* 73 (1960).

––––––. *Sainte Thècle, saints Côme et Damien, saints Cyr et Jean* (extraits), *saint Georges.* Collections grecques des miracles. Paris: Picard, 1971.

Foerster, Werner. "*Eusebeia* in den Pastoralbriefen." *NTS* 5 (1958–59):213–218.

Fustel de Coulanges, Numa Denis. *The Ancient City: A Study on the Religion, Laws, and Institutions of Greece and Rome.* Translated by Willard Small. Doubleday & Co., 1956.

Gager, John G. *Kingdom and Community: The Social World of Early Christianity.*
Prentice-Hall Studies in Religion. Prentice-Hall, 1975.

Gebhardt, Oskar Leopold von. *Passio sanctae Theclae virginis: die lateinischen
Übersetzungen der Acta Pauli et Theclae.* TU, n.s. 7, 2. Leipzig: J. C.
Hinrichs, 1902.

Grant, Mary, tr. and ed. *The Myths of Hyginus.* University of Kansas Publications,
Humanistic Studies 34. University of Kansas Press, 1960.

Gryson, Roger. *The Ministry of Women in the Early Church.* Translated by Jean
Laporte and Mary Louise Hall. Liturgical Press, 1976.

Gunther, John J. *St. Paul's Opponents and Their Background: A Study of Apocalyptic
and Jewish Sectarian Teachings.* Novum Testamentum, Supplement 35. Leiden:
E. J. Brill, 1973.

Hagermann, Harald. "Der geschichtliche Ort der Pastoralbriefe." *Theologische
Versuche* 2 (1970):47–64.

Harnack, Adolf von. *Geschichte der altchristlichen Literatur bis Eusebius.* Part 2: *Die
Chronologie.* 2d ed. Leipzig: J. C. Hinrichs, 1958.

Hennecke, Edgar, and Schneemelcher, Wilhelm, eds. *New Testament Apocrypha.* 2
vols. English translation edited by Robert McL. Wilson. Westminster Press,
1963, 1965.

Herzfeld, Ernest E., and Guyer, Samuel. *Meriamlik und Korykos, zwei christliche
Ruinenstätten des Rauhen Kilikiens.* Monumenta Asiae Minoris Antiqua II.
Manchester: Manchester University Press, for the American Society for
Archaeological Research in Asia Minor, 1930.

Howe, Margaret. "Interpretations of Paul in the Acts of Paul and Thecla." In
Pauline Studies, edited by Donald A. Hagner and Murray J. Harris, pp. 33–49.
Exeter: Paternoster Press, 1980.

The Interpreter's Dictionary of the Bible, Supplementary Volume. Abingdon Press,
1976. S.v. "Cynics," by Abraham J. Malherbe.

Jalabert, Louis, and Mouterde, René, eds. *Inscriptions grecques et latines de la Syria.*
6 vols. Paris: P. Geuthner, 1926–67.

Jansen, William Hugh. "The Esoteric-Exoteric Factor in Folklore." In *The Study
of Folklore*, edited by Alan Dundes, pp. 43–51. Prentice-Hall, 1965.

Jason, Heda. "A Model for Narrative Structure in Oral Literature." In *Patterns in
Oral Literature*, edited by Heda Jason and Dimitri Segal, pp. 99–133. World
Anthropology Series. The Hague: Mouton & Co., 1977.

Jason, Heda, and Segal, Dimitri. "Introduction." In *Patterns in Oral Literature*,
edited by Heda Jason and Dimitri Segal, pp. 1–10. World Anthropology
Series. The Hague: Mouton & Co., 1977.

Jenkins, Claude. "Origen on 1 Corinthians." *JTS* 10 (1908–09):29–51.

Kaestli, Jean-Daniel. "Les Principales Orientations de la recherche sur les Actes
apocryphes." In *Les Actes apocryphes des Apôtres*, edited by François Bovon, pp.
49–67. Publications de la faculté de théologie de l'Université de Genève 4.
Geneva: Labor et Fides, 1981.

Karris, Robert J. "The Background and Significance of the Polemic of the
Pastoral Epistles." *JBL* 92 (1973):549–564.

Knoch, Otto. *Die "Testamente" des Petrus und Paulus: Die Sicherung der apostolischen
Überlieferung in der Spätneutestamentlichen Zeit.* Stuttgart: KBW Verlag, 1973.

Kolbenschlag, Madonna. *Kiss Sleeping Beauty Good-Bye: Breaking the Spell of
Feminine Myths and Models.* Doubleday & Co., 1979.

Kümmel, Werner Georg. *Introduction to the New Testament*. 14th rev. ed. Translated by A. J. Mattill, Jr. Abingdon Press, 1966.

Labriolle, Pierre Champagne de. *La Crise Montaniste*. Paris: Leroux, 1913.

Lawlor, H. J., and Oulton, J. E. L. *Eusebius: The Ecclesiastical History and the Martyrs of Palestine*. 2 vols. London: S.P.C.K., 1954.

Leclercq, Henri. *Les Martyrs*, Vol. 1: *Les Temps Néroniens et le deuxième siècle*. Paris: H. Oudin, 1921.

Lefebvre, Gustave, ed. *Recueil des inscriptions grecques chrétiennes d'Égypte*. Cairo: L'Institute Français d'Archéologie Orientale, 1907.

Lindemann, Andreas. *Paulus im ältesten Christentum. Das Bild des Apostels und die Rezeption der paulinischen Theologie in der frühchristlichen Literatur bis Marcion*. BHT 58. Tübingen: J. C. B. Mohr (Paul Siebeck), 1979.

Lipsius, Richard Adelbert. *Die apokryphen Apostelgeschichten und Apostellegenden. Ein Beitrag zur altchristlichen Literaturgeschichte*. 2 vols. Braunschweig: C. A. Schwetschke und Sohn, 1887.

Lipsius, Richard Adelbert, and Bonnet, Maximilian, eds. *Acta apostolorum apocrypha*, 3 vols. Leipzig: Hermann Mendelsohn, 1891–1903. Reprint. Darmstadt: Wissenschaftliche Buchgesellschaft, 1959.

Lord, Albert B. *The Singer of Tales*. Harvard University Press. Reprint. Atheneum Publishers, 1978.

Lucius, Ernest. *Die Anfänge des Heiligenkults in der christlichen Kirche*. Edited by Gustav Anrich. Tübingen: J. C. B. Mohr (Paul Siebeck), 1904.

MacDonald, Dennis Ronald. "A Conjectural Emendation of 1 Cor 15:31–32: Or the Case of the Misplaced Lion Fight." *HTR* 73 (1980):265–276.

Magie, David. *Roman Rule in Asia Minor to the End of the Third Century After Christ*. 2 vols. Roman History Series. Arno Press, 1975.

Malherbe, Abraham J. *Social Aspects of Early Christianity*. Louisiana State University Press, 1977.

Mayer, Hans Helmut. *Über die Pastoralbriefe*. FRLANT. Göttingen: Vandenhoeck & Ruprecht, 1913.

Meeks, Wayne A. "The Christian Proteus." In *The Writings of St. Paul*, edited by Wayne A. Meeks, pp. 435–444. W. W. Norton & Co., 1972.

Monumenta Asiae Minoris Antiqua. 8 vols. Manchester: Manchester University Press, for the American Society for Archaeological Research in Asia Minor, 1928–62.

Moule, C. F. D. "The Problem of the Pastoral Epistles: A Reappraisal." *BJRL* 47 (1964–65):430–452.

Musurillo, Herbert. *The Acts of the Christian Martyrs: Introduction, Texts and Translations*. London: Oxford University Press, 1972.

Nock, Arthur Darby. *Conversion: The Old and the New in Religion from Alexander the Great to Augustine of Hippo*. Oxford: Clarendon Press, 1933. Reprint. London: Oxford University Press, 1961.

Olrik, Alex. "Epic Laws of Folk Narrative." In *The Study of Folklore*, edited by Alan Dundes, pp. 131–141. Prentice-Hall, 1965.

Osborne, Robert E. "Paul and the Wild Beasts." *JBL* 85 (1966):225–230.

Pagels, Elaine Hiesey. *The Gnostic Paul: Gnostic Exegesis of the Pauline Letters*. Fortress Press, 1975.

Paulsen, H. "Die Bedeutung des Montanismus für die Herausbildung des Kanons." *VC* 32 (1978):19–52.

Prigent, Pierre. "Hérésie asiate et l'église confessante: De l'Apocalypse à Ignace." *VC* 31 (1977):1–22.

Propp, Vladímir. *Morphology of the Folktale.* Translated by Laurence Scott with an introduction by Svatava Pirkova-Jakobson; 2d ed. rev. and ed. with a preface by Louis A. Wagner, and with a new introduction by Alan Dundes. University of Texas Press, 1968.

Radermacher, Ludwig. *Hippolytus und Thekla. Studien zur Geschichte von Legende und Kultus.* Kaiserliche Akademie der Wissenschaften in Wien. Philosophich-historische Klasse. Sitzungsberichte 182, 3. Vienna: Alfred Hölder, 1916.

Ramsay, William Mitchell. "The Acta of Paul and Thekla." In his *The Church in the Roman Empire Before A.D. 170,* pp. 375–428. G. P. Putnam, 1893. Reprint. Baker Book House, 1954.

————. *The Cities and Bishoprics of Phrygia.* 2 vols. Oxford: Clarendon, 1895–97. Reprint. Roman History Series. New York: Arno Press, 1975.

Reinach, Salomon. "Thékla." *Annales du Musée Guimet* 35 (1910):103–140.

Reitzenstein, Richard. *Hellenistische Wundererzählungen.* 3d ed. Stuttgart: B. G. Teubner, 1974.

Rensberger, David K. "As the Apostle Teaches: The Development of the Use of Paul's Letters in Second-Century Christianity." Ph.D. dissertation, Yale University, 1981.

Rist, Martin. "Pseudepigraphic Refutations of Marcionism." *JR* 22 (1942):39–62.

Robinson, James M., ed. *The Nag Hammadi Library in English.* Harper & Row, 1977.

Rohde, Johannes. "Pastoralbriefe und Acta Pauli." In *SE* 5, edited by F. L. Cross, pp. 303–310. TU 103. Berlin: Akademie-Verlag, 1968.

Ruether, Rosemary Radford. "Misogynism and Virginal Feminism in the Fathers of the Church." In *Religion and Sexism: Images of Woman in the Jewish and Christian Traditions,* edited by Rosemary Radford Ruether, pp. 150–183. Simon & Schuster, 1974.

————. "Mothers of the Church: Ascetic Women in the Late Patristic Age." In *Women of Spirit: Female Leadership in the Jewish and Christian Traditions,* edited by Rosemary Ruether and Eleanor McLaughlin, pp. 71–98. Simon & Schuster, 1979.

Schlau, Carl. *Die Acten des Paulus und die ältere Thekla-Legende. Ein Beitrag zur christlichen Literaturgeschichte.* Leipzig: J. C. Hinrichs, 1877.

Schlepelern, Wilhelm E. *Der Montanismus und die phrygischen Kulte. Eine religionsgeschichtliche Untersuchung.* Translated into German from Dutch by W. Bauer. Tübingen: J. C. B. Mohr (Paul Siebeck), 1929.

Schmidt, Carl. *Acta Pauli aus der Heidelberger koptischen Papyrushandschrift Nr. 1.* Leipzig: J. C. Hinrichs, 1905. Reprint. Hildesheim: Georg Olms, 1965.

Schmidt, Carl, and Schubart, Wilhelm. *Praxeis Paulou: Acta Pauli nach dem Papyrus der Hamburger Staats- und Universitäts-Bibliothek.* Glückstadt and Hamburg: J. J. Augustin, 1936.

Shaw, George Bernard. *Androcles and the Lion.* Penguin Plays. Penguin Books, 1963.

Sint, Joseph A. *Pseudonymität im Altertum. Ihre Formen und ihre Gründe.* Commentationes Aenipontanae 15. Innsbruck: Wagner, 1960.

Söder, Rosa. *Die apokryphen Apostelgeschichten und die romanhafte Literatur der*

Antike. Würzburger Studien zur Altertumswissenschaft 3. Stuttgart: W. Kohlhammer, 1932. Reprint. Stuttgart: W. Kohlhammer, 1969.

Souter, A. "The 'Acta Pauli' etc. in Tertullian." *JTS* 25 (1924):292.

Speyer, Wolfgang. *Die literarische Fälschung im heidnischen und christlichen Altertum. Ein Versuch ihrer Deutung.* Handbuch der Altertumswissenschaft 1. Munich: Verlag C. H. Beck, 1971.

––––––. "Religiöse Pseudepigraphie und literarische Fälschung im Altertum." *JAC* 8–9 (1965–66):88–125.

Stenger, Werner. "Timotheus und Titus als literarische Gestalten (Beobachtungen zur Form und Funktion der Pastoralbriefe)." *Kairos* 16 (1974):252–267.

Stevenson, James. *A New Eusebius: Documents Illustrative of the History of the Church to A.D. 337.* Edited by B. J. Kidd. London: S.P.C.K., 1968.

Strobel, August. "Schreiben des Lukas? Zum sprachlichen Problem der Pastoralbriefe." *NTS* 15 (1968–69):191–210.

Strugnell, John. "A Plea for Conjectural Emendation in the New Testament, with a Coda on 1 Cor 4:6." *CBQ* 34 (1974):543–558.

Theissen, Gerd. *Sociology of Early Palestinian Christianity.* Translated by John Bowden. Fortress Press, 1978.

Torm, Friedrich. *Die Psychologie der Pseudonymität im Hinblick auf die Literatur des Urchristentums.* Studien der Luther-Akademie 2. Gütersloh: Bertelsmann, 1932.

Trummer, Peter. *Die Paulustradition der Pastoralbriefe.* BEvT 8. Frankfurt: Peter Lang Verlag, 1978.

Turner Victor. *The Ritual Process: Structure and Anti-Structure.* Aldine Publishing Co., 1969.

Utley, Francis Lee. "Folk Literature: An Operational Definition." In *The Study of Folklore,* edited by Alan Dundes, pp. 7–24. Prentice-Hall, 1965.

Vouaux, Léon. *Les Actes de Paul et ses lettres apocryphes: introduction, textes, traduction et commentaire.* Les apocryphes du Nouveau Testament. Paris: Librairie Letouzey et Ané, 1913.

Walker, William O., Jr. "1 Corinthians 11:2–16 and Paul's Views Regarding Women." *JBL* 94 (1975):94–110.

Walzer, Richard. *Galen on Jews and Christians.* London: Oxford University Press, 1949.

Wendland, Paul. *De fabellis antiquis earumque ad Christianos propagatione.* Göttingen: W. F. Kaestner, 1911.

––––––. *Die urchristlichen Literaturformen.* HNT 1, 3. Tübingen; J. C. B. Mohr, 1912.

Wilson, Stephen G. *Luke and the Pastoral Epistles.* London: S.P.C.K., 1979.

INDEXES

BIBLICAL CITATIONS

OTHER EARLY CHRISTIAN WRITINGS

OTHER ANCIENT AUTHORS

SUBJECTS

PERSONAL NAMES

Place Names

MODERN AUTHORS